First Published on June 14, 2018
(Donald Trump's Birthday is June 14)
Happy Birthday Donald!!!

Trump Is a Duck

QUANTITY PURCHASES: Schools, companies, professional groups, clubs, organizations or individuals may qualify for special terms when ordering quantities of this title. For more information, visit: www.BluntHonest.com

Publisher's Cataloging-in-Publication Data

Names: Honest, Blunt, author.
Title: Trump is a duck : a rabbit hole of narcissism and empathy / created by Blunt Honest.
Description: Denver : PlayVM, 2018.
Identifiers: LCCN 2018952890 | ISBN 978-1-7320633-0-3 (pbk.) | ISBN 978-1-7320633-2-7
    (hardcover) | ISBN 978-1-7320633-3-4 (hardcover) | ISBN 978-1-7320633-4-1 (ebook)
Subjects: LCSH: Trump, Donald, 1946- | United States--Politics and government--2017- |
    Presidents--United States. | Narcissism. | Empathy. | Prejudices. | BISAC: POLITICAL SCIENCE /
    American Government / General. | POLITICAL SCIENCE / Commentary & Opinion.
Classification: LCC E912 .H66 2018 (print) | LCC E912 (ebook) | DDC 973.933--dc23.

PlayVMᴏ♪

Published by PlayVM, LLC
Denver, CO

Contents

Love, Abuse, and 40,000 Videos

The origin of this book began 5 years ago when I fell in love with a woman. She was fun, charming, and beautiful. I thought the world of her, until she turned my world upside down.

As our relationship collapsed, I came to see a different side of her. She became the most toxic, abusive, dishonest person I've ever known. If I had to use one word to describe her, that word would be "evil."

That relationship opened my eyes to different types of personalities and different forms of abuse. After surviving that difficult relationship, I spent a lot of time learning about narcissists and other personality types. That experience also caused me to become fascinated by the dynamics of human nature, and I wanted to learn as much as I could about it. I read extensively on a wide range of topics, and also watched lots of videos on YouTube.

YouTube is like a window into the collective consciousness of the world. Over the past 5 years, I've watched over 40,000 videos on YouTube, and I saved links to around 6,000 of the best videos, and classified them into over 100 different categories.

Then I began arranging those curated videos into films that I call "video montages." I held test screenings and showed my films to friends and strangers to see how they reacted to them. After the screenings, I asked people for feedback and some of those test screenings generated lively discussions. Then I took what I learned from the test screenings and improved my video montages.

They say that a picture is worth a thousand words. If that is true, then a video montage must be worth at least 100,000 words. This book shares links to 33 of my video montages. Each collection of videos provides a different window into our world.

Don't be misled by the modest size of this book, because the words, pictures, and videos offer a tremendous amount of depth. This book is a portal and a time capsule. It is a microcosm of our world. I hope this book changes the world.

I'm Only a Messenger

Whether you like Donald Trump or not, one thing is clear: he is now a part of our lives and he is hard to ignore.

This book will help people to understand the dynamics of narcissism and empathy, and what we can learn about those topics by looking into the life and times of Donald Trump.

When I was younger, I was a big fan of Trump. I read his books and viewed him as a mentor. I watched his Apprentice TV show and I even tried out twice to be on it. Perhaps if Trump had run for President when I was younger, I may have voted for him. But as I got older, I came to realize how narcissists had affected my life. My experiences with narcissists helped to open my eyes and I now view Trump differently.

When I first had the idea for this book, I was planning to create a humorous book. However, as I thought more about it, I realized I wanted to create something more than just a joke book, because the topic is so important. This book is a blend of humor and knowledge. It's around 50 percent satire and cartoons, and 50 percent educational. I wanted this to be a thought provoking book, and also a fun and entertaining one.

Humor can help show that we live in crazy times. Sometimes craziness is caused when people in power do things to distort reality. In this book, I use satire to distort reality. Sometimes by distorting the distorted reality of others, it can help reveal a more accurate view of reality.

Donald Trump often claims that bad stories about him are "fake news," but if somebody made up positive stories about Trump that were not true, would he tell people the positive stories were "fake news?"

The "Fake News" section of this book has headlines and stories showing a kinder, gentler, and more empathetic Trump. The fake news is based on real news stories, but I use satire to twist the news and make it more positive. Perhaps my fake news will help reveal the truth about what is fake and what is real.

Cartoons can help reveal things about politics or life. The tone of my humor is meant to be playful. However, sometimes I will be blunt and honest. I think it's better to be blunt and honest than to be fake and insincere. Humor can help shed light on critical issues. There is often truth imbedded in jokes. Comedians can say things in ways that most people cannot.

Throughout the ages, court jesters were given the freedom to speak their minds and not be harmed. Even rulers who would normally punish others for saying things that offended them allowed the fools of the court to speak their mind without repercussions.

Humor is subjective. What one person finds funny might offend someone else. But sometimes humor needs to 'walk a fine line,' or even cross the line and shock us in order to make a point. Humor is meant to be funny or thought-provoking, but sometimes it falls on deaf ears.

Humor helps us look into a mirror and shows us what we can't change, gives us courage to change what we can, and provides the stupidity to know the difference.

Sometimes, we have to be willing to laugh at ourselves. When it comes to the humor and ideas found in this book, please be kind to the messenger, even if you think that he is a fool.

It seems like it's human nature to persecute people we disagree with, only to realize later their ideas had merit. Innovation, progress, and greatness occur when we give each other the freedom to express our views even though we might not agree with each other.

Several years ago, I heard Warren Buffet say something profound. He said he reads lots of books and also reads books written by people whose ideas he doesn't agree with. He said that a sign of true intelligence is a willingness to consider opposing viewpoints, and weigh and discern the merits of those ideas.

Today, we seem to live in self-fulfilling filter-bubbles that reinforce the beliefs we've already formed. We become comfortable and complacent by only listening to people who are preaching to the choir.

Life should be an adventure where we continuously reinvent ourselves and think outside of our boxes to consider opposing viewpoints and the merits that each person brings to the table. A willingness to live outside one's comfort zone is one of the secrets of success. As the saying goes, minds are like parachutes. They only work if they are open.

This is not only a book about Donald Trump, this is also a book about ourselves. In some ways, Trump is like a mirror, and how you view Trump may be a reflection of yourself.

We tend to project ourselves and our beliefs onto the world to create a view of the world that may or may not have anything to do with reality. Perception is reality and sometimes our perceptions are wrong.

At times this book is humorous, and at times it is serious. My goal is to entertain people as well as inform them. I think this book will resonate with different people in different ways.

Please tell others about this book and post your review and feedback online. Also, please consider giving copies of this book to others. I offer volume discounts on my website for people who order five or more copies. My website is: www.BluntHonest.com

Red Pill or Blue Pill?

"After this, there is no turning back. You take the blue pill—the story ends, you wake up in your bed and believe whatever you want to believe. You take the red pill—you stay in Wonderland, and I show you how deep the rabbit hole goes." - from the movie *The Matrix*

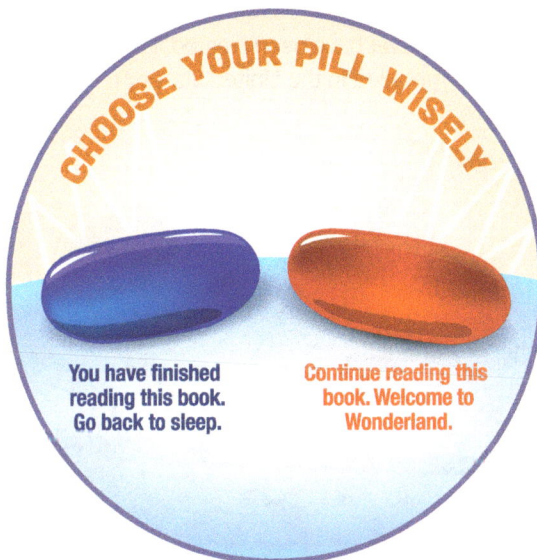

CHOOSE YOUR PILL WISELY

You have finished reading this book. Go back to sleep.

Continue reading this book. Welcome to Wonderland.

Credit for Those Responsible

This book never would have been created if it were not for the individuals who supported and elected Donald Trump.

Trump Supporters

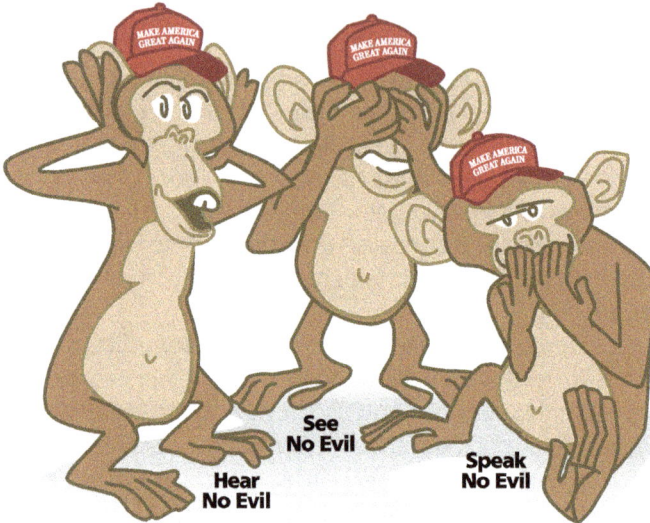

See
No Evil

Hear
No Evil

Speak
No Evil

Trump's Russian Friends

Эта книга, возможно, никогда не была создана, если бы не люди, которые распространяли ложную информацию и вмешивались в президентские выборы в Соединенных Штатах.

(Translation): This book may never have been created if it were not for the individuals who spread false information and meddled in the United States presidential election.

Reasons People Support Trump

Birds of a Feather Theorem

Some people support Trump because they feel they can identify with him. These people may be influenced by the "Birds of a Feather Theorem." This theorem states that birds of a feather flock together.

Economy Fallacy

Some people support Trump because they think he has helped the economy. Trump's economic numbers often get compared to Obama's numbers. However, Obama inherited an economy that was in a severe recession and Trump inherited a much stronger economy.

Trump says he created a lot of jobs. During the first 19 months of Trump's administration, 194,000 new jobs were added per month. However, that growth is less than the 205,000 new jobs per month that were added during the last 19 months Obama was in office. Trump also started a trade war with tariffs that raised prices for consumers and reduced exports. Some companies had to lay off workers or move operations overseas because of his tariffs.

Infinite Trump Theorem

Another reason people supported Trump is that they believed he had the potential to do good things. This belief is based on the "Infinite Trump Theorem." This theorem states that if you lock Donald Trump in a padded room with a monkey on his back, eventually he will do something right.

Golden Touch Fallacy

Some Trump supporters believe he has a golden touch and is infallible. However, at times Trump's success comes at the expense of others. He has been sued by people who worked for him and were not paid. At times, he profits from conflict, notoriety, or factual distortions.

Trump reduced environmental regulations to help some companies. However, it often costs more to solve environmental problems than the profits made from polluting the environment. Taxpayers often pay the costs of environmental damage.

How to Use Video Montages

This book shares links to 33 of my video montages. Video montages are collections of videos that are in YouTube playlists and can be viewed on any device that has access to YouTube. Those playlists share around 800 videos. Some of the videos are amongst the best videos from around the world. The video montages help the pages of this book come alive.

You watch a video montage by going to the website address shown in this book or by scanning the QR-code (QR-Codes are square boxes with dots in them). If you want to scan QR codes, your smart device or smartphone will need a QR-Code scanner app installed. There are many free QR-Code apps available.

If you want to share a video montage with someone else, you can do that by sending them the website address link for the video montage.

The links and QR-codes take you to YouTube. Inside of YouTube, be sure to click on the "Play all" button or link so that YouTube will automatically show you all the videos in the montage, without stopping.

When you are watching a video montage, the first video shows the cover of this book and when you reach the end of the montage, you will see the book cover again. The book covers make it easy to determine when you are at the beginning or end of a montage.

The lengths of video montages vary. Some montages only have a few videos and other montages have more than 50 videos. Most montages can be watched in less than 90 minutes.

Some people may not have time to watch all of the video montages, so I've put priority scores on the video montages to help you decide where to spend your time. Also, some people read for knowledge and others read for entertainment. Sometimes I give two priority scores to help different kinds of readers.

Each video montage has a headline describing the montage. The headline is followed by a priority score shown in parenthesis. I rank things on a scale of 1 to 10 (where 10 is the highest priority). The first number in a priority score indicates the relevancy of the video montage. If there is a second number then it tells you an entertainment score; I don't always show an entertainment score. I only show the entertainment score when it is higher than the relevancy score.

For example, on the next page, the video montage headline is "Orangutan Joke (6,8)." For that montage, the relevancy score is 6, and the entertainment score is 8. So, on a scale of 1 to 10 that montage's relevancy for your understanding of information in this book is a 6. I'm also telling you the montage has a high entertainment value with a score of 8.

You don't need to watch any videos if you don't want to. This book works fine without watching the videos. However, I encourage you to watch the videos because some of them are extraordinary and will add to your depth of experiencing this book.

It's easy to play a video montage. When you go to a link for a montage, videos should automatically play. If videos don't automatically play one after another, then you may want to turn on the autoplay setting in YouTube. You may want to subscribe to YouTube Red (to avoid interruptions from advertisements). At the time I wrote this book, YouTube Red offered a free 30-day trial. Find additional tips about setting up or using YouTube at:

www.BluntHonest.com/Youtube

An Orangutan Joke

For years, Donald Trump questioned the birthplace of Barrack Obama to try to delegitimize Obama's presidency. To be president, a person has to be born an American citizen. Even though Obama released his birth certificate in April, 2011, to prove he was born in Hawaii, that still did not satisfy Trump; he kept demanding more proof.

In 2012, about 2 weeks before the presidential election in which Obama was running for reelection, Trump put a video online saying he wanted further proof of Obama's birth and he offered to donate $5 million to charity if Obama provided that proof.

After Trump made that offer, the comedian Bill Maher joked about this on television and said that he thought Trump's father was probably an orangutan and that he would donate $5 million to charity if Trump proved that his dad was not an orangutan.

A few days later, Trump sent Maher some proof that his father was not an orangutan. Maher was joking when he offered to pay $5 million to charity, but Trump later sued Maher for $5 million for breach of contract. A judge dismissed the lawsuit because normally a joke does not create a binding contract.

Here is a hilarious video montage that shows Trump's $5 million offer to Obama, Bill Maher's orangutan joke, Trump's lawsuit, and jokes about Trump's birther movement.

Orangutan Joke (6,8)
www.BluntHonest.com/Joke

A Deal for Donald

Many of us believe that Donald Trump is a duck. I don't know for sure if it's true. I hope it's not true, but given his feathery hair, his fowl mouth, and the fact he has symptoms of duck syndrome, he must be a duck.

This violates the constitution; ducks cannot be president because they have bird brains. Many people have very serious questions about this and the American people deserve to know, once and for all, if he is a duck.

I have a deal for the president. A deal that I don't believe he can refuse, and I hope he doesn't. If Donald Trump provides his DNA records proving he is not a duck, a comprehensive family tree going back 7 generations, and proof that there are no ducks in his ancestral lineage, then I will make a donation on Donald Trump's behalf of $6.66 to a charity of his choice.

He will be doing a great service for the country if he does this and it will end the questions and quell the anger of many Americans. When he releases his records to my satisfaction, then I will contribute 666 cents on behalf of the president to the charity of his choice. Frankly, this is a contribution I very much want to make. There is one caveat to my offer. Donald Trump must provide me his records within 666 days of the date I first published this book.

Here is a video montage that proves Donald Trump is probably a duck. Also, this montage shows that he may be a dinosaur.

Duck Proof (5,8)
www.BluntHonest.com/Proof

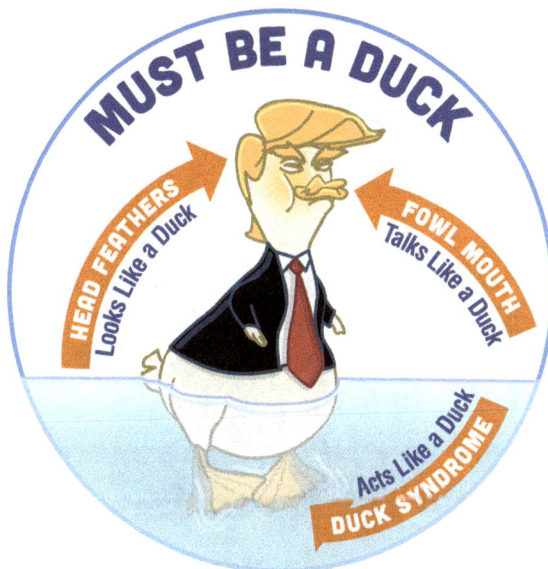

Fake News

Strange news seems to happen weekly with the Trump administration. Sean Spicer was the White House press secretary and sometimes, instead of denying the strange news, he seemed to accept it. At times he was heard saying *"You can't make this shit up."*

South Park creator, Trey Parker, talked about news related to Trump. Parker said *"It's really tricky now as satire has become reality...We were really trying to make fun of what was going on but we couldn't keep up. What was actually happening was way funnier than anything we could come up with. They're already going out and doing the comedy."*

In this next section of my book, I have created some "Fake News" stories. Most of the stories are based on real news stories but have been twisted to portray a kinder, gentler, more empathetic Donald Trump. However, what you will find is that most of the satire in my fake news stories was created by Donald Trump, himself. Trump frequently finds ways to turn reality into satire.

Many of my fake news stories are mostly true, but how I spin and interpret the news is fake. I tried to find positive ways to interpret negative situations. My rose-colored view of a story is where the fake news tends to occur. Often, the only thing fake is the headline. Here are some guidelines to help you know what is real or fake in my news stories:

These things will NOT be fake:
- Statistical information.
- Quotes attributed to people who are named.
- Quotes attributed to a news media source or publication.

These things might be fake:
- Quotes attributed to an anonymous person or an unnamed spokesperson.
- Summaries of what a person said (a person is not directly quoted).
- Interpretations of someone's thoughts, beliefs, or motives.

For example, when I give a person's name and quote them, then those are their actual words. When I quote someone's tweets, I leave any grammar or spelling errors that were in their original tweets. This mostly affect's Trump's tweets which often have grammar and spelling errors.

When I give a person's name and summarize their words, thoughts, or actions but don't quote them directly, then that might be fake news. If I quote someone but don't give the name of the person who is being quoted, then those quotes might be fake.

If you are familiar with the actual news stories, then it should be easy to see what is satirical and what is factual. The fake news tends to be expressed in things that seem like opinions. In one story, I broke one of my guidelines to add to the satire and so I clarified things at the end of that story to tell you what was fake. Also, you can Google the names, quotes, places and events mentioned in my fake news to find the real news stories.

Don't take things too literally in the fake news stories. The stories often use satire and sarcasm to imply the opposite meaning of what the words are saying. Also, sometimes there are stories that will be 100 percent true or 100 percent fake. Some stories build upon other stories to help show irony, reveal character traits, or reveal the moral of a story.

My fake news stories help demonstrate concepts related to empathy or narcissism and provide examples of topics that will be discussed later in this book.

I only twist the news stories in the "Fake News" section of this book. Elsewhere in the book, I am accurate with the facts. I put the words "Fake News" at the top of each page of this chapter to reduce the chances that someone might mistake my fake news as being real news. Also, I used **bold italicized text** for the fake news headlines.

If you are not interested in reading satirical news stories, you can skip ahead to page 52. If you skip ahead, you may still want to read this fake news section later because some of the fake news stories provide information about important world issues, and provide good examples related to empathy or narcissism. The fake news stories begin on the next page.

Trump Wants to be Friends with Kim Jong-un

The leader of North Korea, Kim Jong-un, said that Donald Trump was *"old"* and a *"destroyer"* who *"begged for nuclear war."* Trump sent out a tweet to tell Kim Jong-un that he wanted to be his friend and would never say anything bad about him. Trump tweeted *"Why would Kim Jong-un insult me by calling me "old," when I would NEVER call him "short and fat?" Oh well, I try so hard to be his friend - and maybe someday that will happen!"*

Trump Offers to Help a Smart, Talented Business Woman

In early 2018, numerous news outlets reported that Donald Trump's lawyer paid $130,000 to a porn star named Stormy Daniels shortly before the presidential election. The money was paid to her to be silent about an alleged affair that occurred with her a few months after Trump's wife gave birth to their child in 2006.

Intouch Weekly magazine wrote an article based on an interview they did with Daniels in 2011. According to the article, Trump offered to help her career and he seemed to be interested in having her on his NBC television show *The Apprentice.* Trump told her *"You know what? You're really smart. You're not dumb... You should be on... it would be really, really good for you. People would think you're just this idiot with blond hair and big boobs. You would be perfect for it because you're such a smart businesswoman. You write and you direct and you produce and obviously you're hot and you're beautiful... we have to work on this for you... We have to get together to talk about your appearance on..."*

Trump Tackles Cyber Bullying

Donald Trump may have influenced his wife, First Lady Melania Trump, to make cyber bullying her national cause. After she has solved the cyber-bullying issue, Donald Trump may inspire her to take on other important issues such as misogyny, racism, homophobia, and porn star infidelity.

Trump Cooperates with Russian Probe

Donald Trump is cooperating with Russia to be a Manchurian Candidate.

Trump Helps Puerto Rico Hurricane Victims

Trump went to Puerto Rico to toss rolls of paper towels to the local citizens.

Trump Gives Privacy to a Breastfeeding Mother

When Elizabeth Beck wanted to pump breast milk for her child, Donald Trump left the room. She said *"He got up, his face got red, he shook his finger at me and he screamed, 'You're disgusting, you're disgusting,' and he ran out of there."*

Trump Comes in Third Place

In 2013, Trump tweeted *"If I'm the third most envied man in America, the small group of haters and losers must be nauseas."* Trump's third place standing means that only Jesus Christ, and *People* magazine's "most sexy man alive" are more popular than Trump.

Trump's Inauguration Focuses on Abraham Lincoln's Legacy

On the day of the Presidential inauguration, First Lady, Melania Trump, was asked by a reporter about plans for the day. She said that her husband had chosen the Lincoln Bible to be used at his inauguration swearing-in. Donald Trump was touched by how Abraham Lincoln's inauguration speech had talked about "the better angels of our nature." Here is that part of Lincoln's speech:

> *"We are not enemies, but friends. We must not be enemies. Though passion may have strained, it must not break our bonds of affection. The mystic chords of memory, stretching from every battlefield and patriot grave to every living heart and hearthstone all over this broad land, will yet swell the chorus of the Union, when again touched, as surely they will be, by the better angels of our nature."*

When asked if she knew what her husband was going to say in his inauguration speech, the First Lady shared a copy of his speech with the reporter. Here is what the speech said:

> *"I want to find a way to bring together whites, blacks, Christians, Muslims, Mexicans, the LGBTQ-community, women, men, and immigrants. We are a diverse nation. From our humble beginnings we have welcomed others from many nations, cultures, and religions. Our diversity helps us thrive and is part of what makes America great.*

> *"I appreciate the freedoms we have in this country. The freedom of the press and freedom of speech has been an important principle that has allowed us to have thoughtful discussions. These freedoms have helped us to learn and grow from each other, and also keep each other accountable. I encourage everyone to use these freedoms to make America great.*

> *"Currently, the United States is one of the most dangerous countries in the world because mass murder from gun shootings are common. Yet every time a mass shooting occurs, people in Congress say they are praying for the victims but do nothing to stop the harm to future victims. The rights of people to go to church, school, or a movie theater without the fear of being shot and killed is more important than providing easy gun access for anyone who wants a gun. We need to enact gun control laws to make America safer.*

> *"The United States incarcerates more of its citizens than any other country. We have less than 5% of the world's population, but nearly 25% of the world's prison population. Clearly, we need to reform our justice system.*

> *"We need to make sure health insurance takes care of people's mental health as well as their physical health. Also, I want to encourage Americans to adopt a healthier lifestyle. In particular, we should add more plant-based food to our diets because this can significantly improve people's health and reduce the chances of serious illnesses. Rising health care costs affect everyone and healthy food is often the best medicine. Plant-based food also helps the environment. Today, around 51 percent of greenhouse gasses are caused by the production and use of animal products such as meat, dairy, and fish.*

> *"We must reduce our dependency on fossil fuels. The time has come for us to eliminate tax breaks and subsidies for fossil fuel companies and start charging them a carbon tax to help reduce the pollution and harm they are causing to the environment.*

> *"We also need to make renewable energy a top priority. Climate change is a serious issue and we have a small window of time to deal with this matter before it becomes worse. More funding needs to be put into research to develop and improve renewable energy. Renewable*

energy is not only good for the environment, it will also be good for our economy because that is the direction the world is heading. We need to embrace renewable energy and lead the way to a better future for all of us.

"We need reforms to reduce the large amounts of money that political action committees can spend to influence elections. Our government officials should serve the needs of the people and not be controlled by special interest groups.

"We need to cooperate with countries around the world and let them know that America wants to be a good citizen of the world and we won't focus solely on putting America's interest's first, but rather we will put the world's interests first and do what is right for all the people on the planet Earth.

"All of us need to put aside our foolish pride and prejudices and recognize that we are all part of the human race. We should look for ways to stand on common ground and develop peace, understanding, acceptance, and friendship with our fellow man.

"I believe that all countries of the world need to get rid of their nuclear weapons. Weapons of mass destruction do not make us safer. They put everyone at risk. An irrational decision or an error could kill millions of people at any given moment.

"A world at peace brings many benefits. For example, Costa Rica abolished their military in 1948 and consistently ranks highest in the world's happiness index. Much of that joy comes from their peace dividend. The money they save from not having a military is used to improve the quality of life for their citizens.

"I believe that all countries of the world should drastically reduce or eliminate their militaries and weapons. This will create a world-wide peace dividend that will come from the savings of $1.7 trillion dollars spent each year on weapons and militaries around the world. That money can be used to improve our schools, provide cleaner water and healthier food, develop new technologies, provide more grants for scientific and medical research, improve healthcare, improve infrastructure, increase funding for the arts and culture, and many other things that will benefit mankind.

"The United States should lead the way in reducing our military because we are the most militaristic nation in the world. The USA spends more on defense than the next 8 countries combined. The USA's defense budget represents a third of the world-wide defense spending. This excessive, annual cost adds to our deficit and lowers the quality of life for our citizens. Other countries have lower taxes and are able to provide better health care, education, and other benefits to their citizens because they are not burdened by huge military expenses.

"Finally, I want to open more doors of opportunity so that in America, it won't matter what the color of your skin is or what your gender, orientation, or nationality is, because if you work hard and do the right things, then anything should be possible for you. I hope to be a good role model for others, especially for girls and boys who may want to become the future leaders of our country."

Later that day, Donald Trump gave his inauguration speech and it did not resemble the speech that the First Lady shared with the reporter. The next day, a spokesperson for the White House explained that the First Lady had found a speech written by Michelle Obama and had mistakenly believed it was the inauguration speech for her husband. **

** Editor's note: The speech was not actually written by Michelle Obama. It is part of the fake news of this story. Michelle Obama would probably create a better speech.

Trump Loves People from Norway

It's been reported that in a meeting, Trump said *"Why do we want these people from all these shithole countries here? We should have more people from places like Norway."*

Trump Is Not a Racist

When Trump was asked about his racist comments about "shithole countries", Trump said to reporters *"No, I'm not a racist. I'm the least racist person you will ever interview."*

Trump Calls Out White Supremacists

Trump brought attention to white supremacists in Charlottesville and said *"The press has treated them absolutely unfairly. You also had some very fine people on both sides."*

Trump Stands up for Freedom of Speech

Shortly before the 2018 Super Bowl game, Trump released a statement saying *"We proudly stand for the national Anthem."* In the past, some football players knelt during the national anthem to draw attention to racial injustice and police brutality. Trump used his freedom of speech and said *"Wouldn't you love to see one of these NFL owners, when somebody disrespects our flag, to say, 'Get that son of a bitch off the field right now. Out! He's fired. He's fired!'"*

Trump Says Mexicans Are Good People

In his presidential nomination speech, Trump said *"The US has become a dumping ground for everyone else's problems…When Mexico sends its people, they're not sending their best… They're sending people that have lots of problems, and they're bringing those problems with us. They're bringing drugs. They're bringing crime. They're rapists. And some, I assume, are good people."*

Trump Teaches Linguistic Lessons

At an election rally in Reno, Nevada, Trump tried to impress the crowds by explaining how to properly pronounce the word "Nevada." However, Nevadans became upset as he repeatedly mispronounced the word "Nevada." Then Trump changed the topic to Mexico and he mispronounced the word "Mexicans," by calling them "Murderers."

Trump Says It Would Be a Shame to Beat a Homeless Person

In Boston, Scott and Steve Leader urinated on a sleeping, homeless, Hispanic man, repeatedly punched him, and beat him with a metal pole. Scott told the police *"Donald Trump was right. All these illegals need to be deported."* When asked how he felt about the beating, Trump said *"It would be a shame, but I haven't heard about that…people who are following me are very passionate…they want this country to be great again."*

Trump Bans Terrorists

After Trump put travel restrictions on seven countries, a 5-year-old boy was separated from his mother and detained for 5 hours at the Washington airport. White House spokesperson Sean Spicer explained that no Muslim could be trusted. He said *"…if they are a 5-year-old…maybe they don't pose a threat, but to assume just because of someone's age or gender… that they don't pose a threat would be misguided and wrong."*

Trump Praises Foreign-Aid Workers in Africa, Encourages Long Commitments

During the Ebola crisis, Trump tweeted *"The U.S. cannot allow EBOLA infected people back. People that go to far away places to help out are great – but must suffer the consequences!"*

Trump Resolves Univision's Concerns

Univision had agreed to pay $13.5 million for a five-year deal to broadcast *Miss USA* and *Miss Universe* to Spanish-language audiences. After Trump made disparaging remarks about Mexicans, Univision decided not to broadcast his shows. Trump sued the network for $500 million in damages. They settled out of court.

Trump Visits a First Grade Class

Donald Trump took time out of his busy election campaign to visit first-grade students and teachers at the International Christian Academy in Nevada. After exchanging pleasantries such as *"Does everybody love school?"* he graciously accepted a gift of a holy Bible from a young African-American girl and he hugged her. After the class did a pledge of allegiance to the Bible, Trump taught a geography class that focused on the "Shithole" nations of the world.

Then Trump went to the gym where students and teachers had gathered; Trump said he was amazed by the size of the crowd. He said no other candidate draws as large of crowds that come to see him. After Trump finished his speech, the mostly empty gymnasium cleared out.

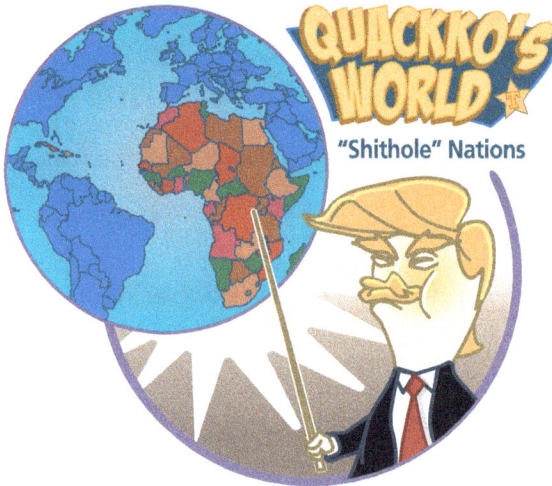

QUACKKO'S WORLD
"Shithole" Nations

Trump Shows Restraint After School Shooting

Normally, when an act of terrorism occurs, Trump uses the actions of one person to justify restrictions on people who belong to the same group as the terrorist. For example, if a terrorist is Muslim, then Trump thinks all Muslims are bad and they need to be restricted and deported.

On Feb 14, 2018, Nikolas Cruz killed 17 people at a Florida high school. Investigators found messages that Cruz had posted online. His words showed hatred towards blacks, Jews, and immigrants. He said he wanted to kill Mexicans. Cruz was a fan of Donald Trump and bragged about writing to Trump and receiving a response. Cruz also liked to wear a "Make America Great Again" hat. After the shooting, Trump did not demand any restrictions or deportations of Trump supporters.

Trump Says Abraham Lincoln Is Still Number One

At an election rally in Youngstown, Ohio, Donald Trump said, *"With the exception of the late, great, Abraham Lincoln, I can be more presidential than any president who has ever held this office."* Then Trump said *"I'd ask whether or not you think I will someday be on Mount Rushmore, but here's the problem. If I did it joking — totally joking, having fun — the fake news media will say, 'He believes he should be on Mount Rushmore.' So I won't say it, okay? I won't say it."*

The crowd was amazed by how masterfully Trump said what he wanted to say and then claimed that he would not say it. The crowd also appreciated Trump's reverence for the sanctity of preserving a national monument for future generations to enjoy.

Trump Gives More Power to Local Citizens

The Trump administration has done the largest rollback of federal land protection in the nation's history. These changes affect national monuments. In Utah, the Bears Ears national monument protected land was reduced by 85 percent and another monument, Grand Staircase-Escalante, was reduced to half its size.

Trump announced the rollback of federal land protection at a speech in Utah. He said he felt the local people are better able to determine if they want to protect that land for future generations or make lots and lots of money by selling that land to filthy-rich real estate developers. Mr. Trump, who happens to be a filthy-rich real estate developer, did not indicate if he plans to buy any of the land that was no longer protected.

This bold move by Trump demonstrates his focus on the future needs of the world rather than being stuck in the past. The land he removed from protection may have up to 100,000 sites of archaeological importance that are no longer important enough to stand in the way of filthy-rich real estate developers.

Also, this move was seen as a victory for fossil fuel companies who may want to exploit the resources of this pristine land. It is not known how much "clean coal" is available in the land, but it is important to note that earlier in the year the Trump administration told the world that clean coal would help solve climate change.

Trump Is Now the Greatest President

At a press conference in February, 2018, Donald Trump announced that he is now considered to be *"The Greatest single president in the history of our country."* Trump based this announcement on a conversation he had with Senator Orrin Hatch who praised Trump and told Trump that he was even better than Abraham Lincoln and George Washington. Following the announcement, Trump said that he loves Senator Hatch.

The next day, Matt Whitlock, a spokesperson for Senator Hatch clarified the conversation Senator Hatch had with the president. Whitlock said *"He has not said that President Trump is the greatest president in the history of our country but that he could be."*

Senator Hatch's words may have been based on the Infinite Trump Theorem. That theorem states that Trump has huge potential if he is locked in a padded room with a monkey on his back and is given an infinite amount of time. Theoretically, Trump could become a greater writer than William Shakespeare, a better basketball player than Michael Jordan, a better singer than Elvis Presley, and a smarter genius than Albert Einstein.

Lincoln's Greatness Rises to the Top

The 2018 Presidents and Executive Politics Presidential Greatness Survey has ranked Abraham Lincoln as being the best president. This survey polled 170 political scientists and asked them to score the "overall greatness" of all United States Presidents using a scale of zero to a hundred where a hundred is the highest score.

According to the survey, the seven greatest presidents listed in order of greatness are: Abraham Lincoln, George Washington, Franklin D. Roosevelt, Theodore Roosevelt, Thomas Jefferson, Harry S. Truman and Dwight Eisenhower.

These presidential experts ranked Donald Trump as being the worst president, ever. Lincoln achieved a greatness score of 95.03 and Trump's greatness score was 12.34.

Trump Is Concerned About the Plight of Birds

Donald Trump has repeatedly criticized wind turbines as being ugly bird-killing machines. He first became concerned about this when the country of Scotland wanted to put wind turbines in the ocean. He was upset how those wind turbines would affect the view from his golf course. Trump wrote letters to the head of the Scottish government where he called the wind turbines "monsters" and described them as "insanity."

It appears that Trump may have been influenced by a novel called *Don Quixote,* where the main character is insane and he thinks that windmills are monsters.

Trump is a big proponent of "clean coal" and claims it will help solve climate change, even though coal power kills 24 times more birds than wind turbines each year.

The man-made structures that kill the most birds are glass buildings. Glass buildings, such as the Trump Tower, kill 3,000 times more birds per year than wind turbines. Around a billion birds die each year when they collide with glass buildings.

The Audubon Society says that the single biggest threat to birds is climate change. Climate change harms bird habitats and climate change may endanger half the birds in the U.S. by the end of the century. One of the best ways to reduce climate change is to reduce our use of fossil fuels by converting to renewable energy sources such as wind power.

Not only are birds affected by pollution caused by fossil fuels, people are also affected. The environmental harm from coal power causes 800,000 premature human deaths worldwide each year. The World Health Organization (WHO) produced estimates of human deaths caused for every trillion kW of electricity produced; these statistics account for environmental health affects as well as workplace safety accidents. According to WHO, the human deaths per trillion

kW, broken down by industry, are: 100,000 deaths from coal power; 36,000 deaths from oil electricity; 4,000 deaths from natural gas; 1,400 deaths from hydro; 440 deaths from rooftop solar; 150 deaths from wind power; 40 deaths from nuclear power.

The Trump administration continues to do things to try to reduce the growth of renewable energy such as putting tariffs on solar panel imports and reducing government funding of renewable energy research.

Meanwhile, the Trump administration continues to promote fossil fuels. The Trump administration is lifting bans on offshore oil drilling and opening billions of acres in the Arctic and other coastal waters; the oil and gas industry kills 3 times more birds per year than wind turbines.

The Trump administration allowed a barrel tax on crude oil to expire in order to give additional tax breaks to oil companies. Fossil fuel industries continue to be heavily subsidized by government tax breaks, and incentives to help fossil fuel companies compete with lower cost renewable energy.

In addition, fossil fuel companies continue to be given exemptions to the Clean Air Act and Clean Water Act so that they are able to pollute the environment. If fossil fuel industries were required to be as clean as renewable energy, it would be too costly for anyone to purchase coal, oil, gasoline or natural gas.

Perhaps the Trump administration fears that if the public switched to renewable energy, the improvements to environmental health may have a harmful effect on big pharmaceutical companies because healthier people don't need to buy drugs to treat illnesses such as asthma, bronchitis, cancer, pneumonia, and other chronic illness.

The Environmental Protection Agency estimates that fossil fuels cause up to $886.5 billion dollars in medical expenses each year in the United States. If people become healthier, this may affect the economy because the health care costs related to using fossil fuels make up around 6% of GDP. The funeral industry would also suffer losses if people were healthier.

In addition, a healthier population may increase unemployment rates because each year in the U.S., employees take off 5.13 million sick days and 26.3 million restricted work days because of illnesses caused by fossil fuels. If people were healthier and more productive, then fewer employees would be needed to cover for the sick and unproductive employees, and this would cause more unemployment.

Perhaps Donald Trump would be more concerned about ugly bird-killing, people-killing coal-fired power plants and oil rigs if they were visible from Trump's golf courses.

Trump Praises Coal in Windy State

Donald Trump visited Cedar Rapids, Iowa in June, 2017 to promote the benefits of coal. Trump cautioned the residents about setting their hopes too high on wind. He said *"I don't want to just hope the wind blows to light up your homes."* Trump also warned the Iowa residents that windmills kill birds. Then he promoted coal as a solution to solve the problem created by Iowa's bird-killing, monster windmills.

Iowa is the leading wind producing state in the United States. Wind power produces 36.6% of the state's electricity. Iowa's last coal mine closed in 1994.

Next, Trump plans to go to Idaho and convince them to stop growing potatoes, then he is going to Florida to discourage farmers from growing oranges. After that he will visit Boston to convince people to become Yankee fans.

Trump Reveals His Wisdom

Over the years, Donald Trump has often said he is smart. He tweeted *"Sorry losers and haters, but my I.Q. is one of the highest – and you all know it! Please don't feel so stupid or insecure, it's not your fault."* At a South Carolina rally he said *"I'm very highly educated. I know words. I have the best words."* When Trump was asked who his advisors were he said *"I'm speaking with myself, number one, because I have a very good brain."*

At a gathering at the CIA (Central Intelligence Agency), Trump showed everyone that he was the smartest person in the room when he said *"Is Donald Trump an intellectual? Trust me, I'm, like, a smart person."* When it was reported that Secretary of State Rex Tillerson called Trump a "moron" and said that Trump lacked a grasp of foreign policy, Trump said *"I guess we'll have to compare IQ tests. And I can tell you who is going to win."*

In January of 2018, when a book questioned Trump's mental fitness, Trump tweeted *"Actually, throughout my life, my two greatest assets have been mental stability and being, like, really smart. Crooked Hillary Clinton also played these cards very hard and, as everyone knows, went down in flames. I went from VERY successful businessman, to top T.V. Star...to President of the United States (on my first try). I think that would qualify as not smart, but genius....and a very stable genius at that!"*

Trump Has Legendary Memory

Donald Trump said he has *"one of the great memories of all time."* However, sometimes his memory seems to lapse. When testifying under oath on two occasions for lawsuits against Trump University, he said *"I don't remember"* 59 times.

Trump may be inflicted with Russian Amnesia. This condition occurs when a person realizes that telling the truth will get them in trouble and telling a lie will also get them in trouble. Russian Amnesia was first discovered when the FBI determined the Russians had interfered with the 2016 election, and many people involved with Trump forgot meetings or conversations they had with the Russians.

Trump Has the Highest IQ

Donald Trump stated in a retweet that his IQ is "the highest" IQ possible. His retweet was in response to someone on Twitter who asked Trump to prove his IQ:

> "@newnonny:@realDonaldTrump @sroyboyk prove it. And while you're at it, prove your alleged IQ as well." The highest, asshole! - June 29, 2013

If Trump has the highest IQ, then this means his IQ is higher than William James Sidis who had an IQ score in the range of 250-300. At the age of 5, Sidis was able to use a typewriter and he knew how to speak Latin, Greek, Russian, French, German, and Hebrew.

It is not known if Trump based his "highest" IQ statement on his actual IQ or if it's based on the Infinite Trump Theorem which states if you lock Donald Trump in a padded room with a monkey on his back and give Trump an infinite amount of time to randomly strike the keys of a typewriter, then theoretically Trump will become fluent in at least 20 different languages.

Trump Becomes Focus of Intelligence Reports

Donald Trump is known to have a short attention span and has difficulty reading intelligence reports. Officials close to Trump have revealed tactics they use to help Trump stay engaged so that he will read the intelligence reports.

The most important thing is to frequently mention Donald Trump's name in the reports. He becomes much more interested in reading intelligence reports if the focus of the report seems to be about him. In addition, most reports need to be summarized on one page and that page needs to be mostly pictures and maps. Trump doesn't like to read and he believes that anything important can be summarized in one page or less.

Trump Has Read All the Classics

Donald Trump says he attended the best schools and was an avid reader who has read all the classics of literature. When asked what his favorite books were, Trump said he especially enjoyed *CliffsNotes on Orwell's Animal Farm* and *SparkNotes on The Odyssey*.

Trump Writes Like Hemmingway

Trump said *"I understand social media...Maybe better than anybody, ever... Somebody said I'm the Ernest Hemingway of 140 characters."* Perhaps Trump's "Somebody" was comparing Trump's writing to Hemmingway's first drafts. Hemmingway said *"The first draft of anything is shit."* Trump's tweets often have grammar errors and misspellings as well as logic and factual errors. Sometimes his tweets seem meaningless, such as when he tweeted *"Despite the constant negative press covfefe"*

Trump Made Speechless by a Generous Offer from Guggenheim

In September of 2017, the Trump administration asked the Guggenheim Museum if it could borrow the 1888 Vincent van Gogh painting "Landscape with Snow" to be placed in Trump's private residence at the White House.

Nancy Spector, the museum's chief curator, was unable to withdraw such a valuable painting from the public, but she made a generous counter offer. She said the Trump White House could borrow a sculpture called "America" by artist Maurizio Cattelan. This is a solid gold functioning toilet valued at over $1 million. The artist, Cattelan, says he creates "1 percent art for the 99 percent." His toilet is a form of satire showing the excessive wealth of some Americans.

Spector's offer seemed appropriate. After all, Trump decorated his living quarters in Trump Tower with an opulent display of gold. Also, this offer seemed timely because of recent news stories about "shithole" countries and a report about a golden shower dossier. The Guggenheim Museum received no response from the White House regarding their generous offer.

Guggenheim Museum Attracts Droves of Trump Supporters

After the Guggenheim museum offered to loan Donald Trump a golden toilet, Trump supporters quickly provided their two cents worth of opinions by posting over 33,000 one-star reviews for the museum on Facebook. The Yelp app was also overwhelmed by Trump Supporters leaving one-star reviews.

It is believed that most of these people have never set foot in an art museum and were jealous that the museum offered Trump a valuable golden toilet but offered nothing to the 99% of Americans who could really benefit from having a solid gold toilet.

Trump Administration Cleans up Government Language

The Trump administration has removed numerous offensive words from government websites and documents. *The Washington Post* reported that the banned words include: "vulnerable," "diversity," "entitlement," "transgender," "fetus," "evidence-based," and "science-based."

Trump Administration Cleans up Wasteful Spending

The Washington Post reports that the 2019 Trump budget is slashing the Department of Energy Funding by 72 percent. The funding earmarked for renewable energy is being reduced. This move came days after Trump expressed wishes to support the growth of fossil fuels such as "clean coal."

Trump Administration Reduces Junk Science

According to the nonprofit Environmental Data & Governance Initiative (EDGI), under the Trump administration, government websites such as the EPA are removing and reducing website content talking about climate change.

The word "climate change" is being replaced with vaguer words such as "sustainability" or "resiliency." The Trump administration doesn't consider climate change a national threat. Scientists have reported they have to avoid putting words like "climate change" in grant requests because it reduces the chances of getting government funding for their projects.

Trump Administration Rejects a Climate Denier

The Trump Administration had nominated Kathleen Hartnett White to lead the Council on Environmental Quality. That job would be responsible for coordinating environmental policy in the various agencies of the executive branch of government.

Hartnett is a known climate denier who says carbon dioxide is the *"gas of life"* and had denied climate change is happening, but later changed her stance to say she wasn't sure if humans had anything to do with it.

She has called renewable energy *"unreliable and parasitic,"* said climate change is *"a creed, a faith, a dogma that has little to do with science"* and has also indicated policies are not dictated by science. According to *NPR*, her book suggested that fossil fuels helped to end slavery.

She was unable to answer basic fundamental questions related to science and the environment such as what percentage of atmospheric heat is stored in the ocean (the answer is 93%). The New York Times has reported that it appears she will not pass the scrutiny of the nomination process and so the Trump White House is planning to withdraw its nomination of her.

Trump Saves American Solar Panel Industry

The Trump Administration made a move to protect United States solar panel manufacturers by putting tariffs of 30 percent on the import of solar panels from other countries.

Critics pointed out that many jobs in the solar industry in the U.S. would be harmed by this decision, because the $28 billion solar industry relies on 80 percent of the panels being imported. This cost will also hinder the adoption and competitiveness of solar panels by adding a tax that increases their cost while at the same time fossil fuel companies continue to receive tax breaks that have subsidized the carbon polluting industries for many decades.

In the USA there are currently 8,000 jobs in the manufacturing of solar panels and 374,000 people employed in the solar energy workforce. The Solar Energy Industries Association (SEIA) estimates that a tariff on solar panels to protect the manufacturing jobs could cost 88,000 jobs in the solar energy workforce in the U.S. SEIA President and CEO Abigail Ross Hopper said *"Rather than help the industry, the action would kill many thousands of American jobs and put a stop to billions of dollars in private investment."*

Trump Embraces Climate Change

When cold weather hit the East Coast in December, 2017, Trump tweeted *"In the East, it could be the COLDEST New Year's Eve on record. Perhaps we could use a little bit of that good old Global Warming that our Country, but not other countries, was going to pay TRILLIONS OF DOLLARS to protect against, Bundle up!"*

Scott Pruitt, the man who Trump appointed as head of the Environmental Protection Agency (EPA) is also embracing climate change. In a television interview he said, *"We know that humans have most flourished during times of, what? Warming trends. So, I think there's assumptions made that because the climate is warming, that that necessarily is a bad thing...I think it's pretty arrogant for people in 2018 to say, 'you know, we know what the ideal surface temperature should be in the year 2100.'"*

However, scientists disagree with Pruitt and say it is better to maintain the temperature that humans and most of the existing life on Earth has evolved to thrive in. Small changes in temperature can melt glaciers and cause large areas of land to be covered with water. Climate change may cause many plants and animals to go extinct.

When Trump nominated Pruitt to lead the EPA, the nomination statement justified his nomination, and claimed the EPA currently had an "anti-energy agenda that has destroyed millions of jobs." During the nomination approval process, Gene Karpinski, president of League of Conservation Voters, warned that putting Pruitt in charge of the EPA was *"like the fox guarding the henhouse... Time and again, he has fought to pad the profits of Big Polluters at the expense of public health."*

After Pruitt was confirmed to run the EPA, it was discovered he had close ties to ALEC, an organization funded by Koch Industries and others who have an interest in promoting the interests of fossil fuel industries. Pruitt has rolled back many of regulations that reduced pollution to the environment. He is going to rename the organization to better reflect its change in focus. "EPA" will now stand for "Environmental Pollution Agency."

Trump Comes to the Rescue

After Hurricane Harvey killed at least 40 people and displaced many families, President Trump did his best to cheer up the survivors at an emergency center in Houston. When he arrived at the center, Trump was impressed by the size of the crowd of 1,000 people who were displaced from their flooded homes. He seemed to think all those people were at the center mainly to greet him. Trump said *"What a crowd! What a turnout!"*

He did high fives with the children and he told jokes. He wanted to make sure people knew he had "big hands." One child was wearing a shirt that said, "Trump is my president", and Donald pulled the child out from the crowd and put him in front of the television cameras. Trump said, *"Look at this guy. You just became famous."*

Trump congratulated everyone for doing a good job and said, *"As tough as this was, it's been a wonderful thing."* As Trump left the homeless survivors he smiled and said *"Have a good time, everyone."* In spite of the tragedy and loss of life, Trump seemed very upbeat. The minimal interactions he had with the residents were lighthearted and fun. Trump talked mostly about how amazing and record breaking the hurricane was.

Trump returned to the Houston shelter 4 days later to hand out hot dogs and potato chips. By now the crowd had grown to 1,200 people. Trump congratulated himself as he talked with reporters saying, *"They're really happy with what's going on...It's something that's been very well received. Even by you guys, it's been very well received."*

Some have said that Trump had so much fun visiting areas with destroyed homes that he is thinking about redeveloping abandoned neighborhoods around the country by flooding them and turning them into urban water parks, to let others experience the joy of visiting a flood zone.

Trump Congratulates Himself on Behalf of the Dead

On May 28, 2018, Trump tweeted *"Happy Memorial Day! Those who died for our great country would be very happy and proud at how well our country is doing today. Best economy in decades, lowest unemployment numbers for Blacks and Hispanics EVER (& women in 18 years), rebuilding our Military and so much more. Nice!"*

Trump's Advisory Board (Shown Left) and His Chief Strategist

Trump Explains What It Means to Be a Hero

Donald Trump spent five years going to a private New York military academy. When he was old enough to get drafted, Trump received FIVE draft deferments. Four times he was deferred for going to college. Once he got out of college, a doctor deferred him for bone spurs in his heel. Around the time of his medical deferment, Trump was active in many sports including football, squash, baseball, and tennis.

Even though Trump never served in the military, he said *"I felt that I was in the military in the true sense because I dealt with those people."* Trump credits his personal life experiences for helping him understand what it is like to serve in the military. In 1997, on *The Howard Stern Show*, Trump talked about sexually transmitted diseases and said, *"I've been so lucky in terms of that whole world. It is a dangerous world out there – it's scary, like Vietnam. Sort of like the Vietnam era. It is my personal Vietnam. I feel like a great and very brave soldier."*

Arizona Senator John McCain had a much different set of military experiences. McCain was a naval aviator in the Vietnam War. During a bombing mission his plane was shot down. When McCain ejected from his plane, he broke his arms and a leg and was knocked unconscious. McCain regained consciousness when his parachute landed him in a lake and he managed to activate his life preserver with his teeth.

Soon after he crashed, McCain was pulled out of the water by the Vietnamese. They fractured his shoulder by hitting it with a rifle and they stabbed his abdomen and foot with a bayonet. They interrogated him for several days and put him in solitary confinement. When the Vietnamese found out he was the son of an admiral, they tried to use him as propaganda by offering to let him go free. McCain refused their offer and said he would only do what they wanted if they released every man who was captured before him

After he refused to cooperate, they beat him every few hours. His left arm was broken again and his ribs were cracked. Eventually the torture made him feel suicidal and he agreed to write a confession. Looking back at that decision McCain said *"I felt just terrible about it... Every man has his breaking point. I had reached mine."* He spent five-and-a-half years as a prisoner of war. McCain received numerous military awards including two Purple Heart medals and a Silver Star. His war injuries made him walk with a limp for the rest of his life.

While campaigning for president, Trump said McCain is *"...not a war hero. He was a war hero because he was captured. I like people who weren't captured."*

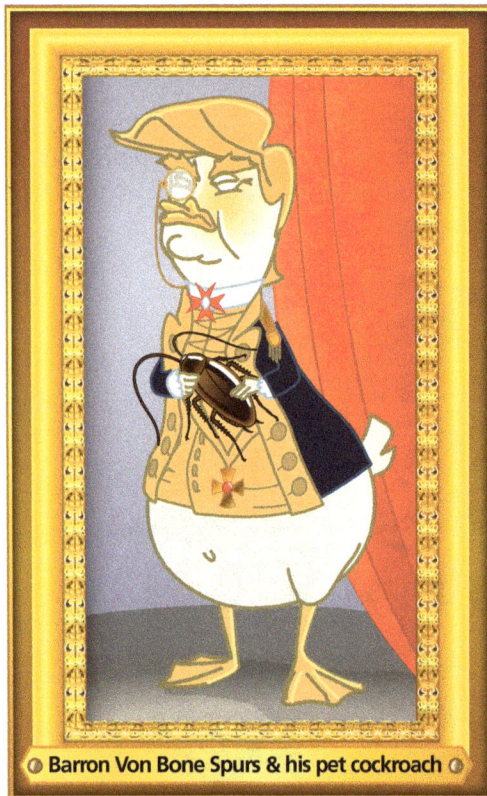

● Barron Von Bone Spurs & his pet cockroach ●

Trump Regrets His Tweet

In 2014, Kim Novak, a Hollywood movie star, made a rare appearance at the Academy Awards. When Trump saw her on television, he tweeted *"I'm having a real hard time watching the Academy Awards (so far). The last song was terrible! Kim should sue her plastic surgeon!"* His tweet devastated her and for months she was unable to go out in public. In 2015, Trump said he regretted that tweet. He said *"I would have preferred I didn't send it. That was done in fun, but sometimes you do things in fun and they turn out to be hurtful."* Novak said she accepted Trump's apology and said, *"It's too bad that bullies don't think before they open their mouths."*

Trump Says Killings Were Unnecessary

On January 7, 2015, Two Islamic gunman killed 12 people who worked at the French satirical magazine Charlie Hebdo. A week after the shootings, Trump tweeted *"Charlie Hebdo reminds me of the "satirical" rag magazine Spy that was very dishonest and nasty and went bankrupt. Charlie was also broke! If the morons who killed all of those people at Charlie Hebdo would have just waited, the magazine would have folded - no money, no success!"*

Congress Trusts God

Whenever mass shootings occur in the United States, lawmakers offer their thoughts and prayers to the victims. Nothing is done to solve the problem. After each new slaughter occurs, lawmakers offer more thoughts and prayers to the victims. Congress has recently announced that all branches of law enforcement and the military are being eliminated including the FBI, CIA, and TSA. National security is being replaced by thoughts and prayers.

Trump's Presidential Aspirations

In 1990, while he was being interviewed by *Playboy* magazine, Trump said: *"I don't want to be President. I'm 100 percent sure."* The book *Fire and Fury* (Henry Holt and Co, 2018) said that Trump didn't expect to be president and he planned to lose the election. The goal wasn't to win, but rather Trump wanted to be the most famous man in the world and he could leverage that fame into other business opportunities.

Trump's friend, Roger Ailes, the former head of *Fox News*, liked to tell people that a great way to have a career in television is to first run for President. According to an article in *New York* magazine, there were rumors that Trump was looking into creating a Trump television network as the election approached, and the expectation was that he would lose the election. Losing a presidential election would help Trump attract an audience for his new network. He could then claim to be a victim of an "unfair election" and be an outspoken critic of President Hillary Clinton. This may have worked if he had lost the election. But now he has to put his network plans on hold and do a job he wasn't expecting to have.

Trump's Campaign Was Similar to a Movie

Some people are comparing Trump's presidential campaign to the movie *The Producers*. That movie is about a dishonest man who has passed his glory days. He comes up with a scheme to make a lot of money by intentionally producing a Broadway show that flops. He oversells shares of investments in his new show and plans to keep that money because nobody expects their investment back when a play fails. His plan backfires when his show is successful. Eventually his fraud is discovered and he ends up in jail.

Trump Is a Broadway Critic and a Mind Reader

In November of 2016, Vice-President-elect Mike Pence attended the Broadway musical Hamilton. At the end of the play, an actor acknowledged that Pence was in the audience and the actor said *"We had a guest in the audience this evening...Vice President Pence, we welcome you and we truly thank you for joining us here at 'Hamilton: An American Musical.' ... We are the diverse America who are alarmed and anxious that your new administration will not protect us, our planet, our children, our parents, or defend us and uphold our inalienable rights. But, we truly hope that this show has inspired you to uphold our American values and to work on behalf of all of us."*

Later, Donald Trump tweeted *"Our wonderful future V.P. Mike Pence was harassed last night at the theater by the cast of Hamilton, cameras blazing. This should not happen! The Theater must always be a safe and special place. The cast of Hamilton was very rude last night to a very good man, Mike Pence. Apologize!"* The next day, Trump tweeted *"The cast and producers of Hamilton, which I hear is highly overrated, should immediately apologize to Mike Pence for their terrible behavior"* A couple days later, Pence told *Fox News "I really enjoyed watching Hamilton. It was a real joy to be there."*

Trump Whitehouse Is Like a Movie

Some people are comparing Trump's presidency to the movie *Wag the Dog*. In that movie, the United States president is caught in a sex scandal and he creates a fake conflict to distract the press from reporting on the sex scandal.

NRA Changes Name To NSAARA

The NRA has changed its name to the National Semi-Automatic Assault Rifle Association. A spokesperson for NSAARA said *"We were founded to support hunters, but increasingly humans are the ones being hunted. Today, you don't want to take a rifle to a semi-automatic gun fight because you will likely die. In America, it is easy to obtain guns and so it is imperative for anyone over the age of 16 to own at least one semi-automatic rifle that can fire up to 120 rounds per minute.*

"Our new name better reflects our purpose. The NSAARA will help increase the profits of gun manufacturers and body armor companies. Currently, the USA spends around $100 billion per year on the cost of gun shootings. Most of that cost is paid for by taxpayer dollars for police, prison, and prosecution efforts. Around $2.8 billion per year is paid for medical expenses of people who are injured by guns. Gunshots are the third leading cause of injuries in the U.S. The economic impact of gun violence is higher if you consider other factors such as loss of property values and reduction of business opportunities in areas prone to gun violence.

"The economic value of gun violence far exceeds the $13.5 billion spent each year on guns and ammunition. By encouraging more people to own semi-automatic guns, we anticipate the economic impact from gun shootings will increase significantly. This will not only help gun manufacturers, but will also help lawyers, doctors, therapists, hospitals, artificial limb manu-facturers, wheelchair companies, long-term care facilities, funeral industries, and police and security industries.

"There are currently around 270 million to 310 million guns in the U.S. (about one gun per person). We want to increase gun sales in a saturated market and so we will be increas-ing our fear-based campaigns to encourage people to replace their outdated guns with more

lethal weapons. Also, we will convince people that owning a gun is a good idea even though households with guns are 3 times more likely to have someone commit suicide and are twice as likely to have a victim of homicide."

Trump Offers Condolences to Arianna Huffington

Donald Trump tweeted *"@ariannahuff is unattractive both inside and out. I fully understand why her former husband left her for a man - he made a good decision."* – August 28, 2012

Trump waited 15 years to provide his analysis of her failed marriage. Arianna and her husband split up in 1997. He sent his tweet after the *Huffington Post* published a story that had the headline "Donald Trump: Why so Moody?"

Trump Is Well-Endowed

After Marco Rubio said that Trump had small hands, Trump raised his hands and said *"Look at those hands, are they small hands?...And, he referred to my hands -- 'if they're small, something else must be small.' I guarantee you there's no problem. I guarantee."*

Trump's Chivalry

In an *Access Hollywood* recording, before meeting a female reporter, Trump said *"I got to use some Tic–Tacs, just in case I start kissing her. You know I'm automatically attracted to beautiful...I just start kissing them, it's like a magnet. Just kiss. I don't even wait."*

Trump Understands Women

In an *Access Hollywood* recording, Trump said *"When you're a star, they let you do it. You can do anything. Grab them by the pussy... can do anything."*

Trump Honors Marriage, Fidelity

In an *Access Hollywood* recording, Trump said *"I moved on her actually, you know she was down in Palm Beach. I moved on her, and I failed, I'll admit it. I did try and fuck her, she was married... and I moved on her very heavily. In fact, I took her furniture shopping. She wanted to get some furniture, I said I'll show you where they have some nice furniture. I took her furniture... I moved on her like a bitch! I couldn't get there, and she was married. And all the sudden I see her and she now has the big phony tits and everything. She's totally changed her look."*

How Donald Trump Respects Women

God's Gift to Women

FLAT DONALD'S WORLDWIDE ADVENTURES

Hey Kids! (and kids at heart)

33 USA

Send Flat Donald on a trip around the world!

Color and decorate Flat Donald, cut him out and send him to your friends and family throughout the world! Ask them to take Flat Donald to their favorite places and take photos to post online and share with you and others so that everyone can see the fun that Flat Donald had.

Photograph and share this image or visit **www.DuckPrez.com/Flat** for pictures of Flat Donald you can print and share.

DUCKPREZ.com

FLAT DONALD'S WORLDWIDE ADVENTURES

DUCKPREZ.com

Trump Apologizes for Access Hollywood Recording

When the *Access Hollywood* recording came out prior to the elections, Trump made a video to apologize. His video said *"I've never said I'm a perfect person, nor pretended to be someone that I'm not. I've said and done things I regret, and the words released today on this more than a decade–old video are one of them. Anyone who knows me, know these words don't reflect who I am. I said it, it was wrong, and I apologize."*

Then Trump reassured everyone about how great he is by saying *"I've travelled the country talking about change for America. But my travels have also changed me. I've spent time with grieving mothers who've lost their children, laid-off workers whose jobs have gone to other countries, and people from all walks of life who just want a better future. I have gotten to know the great people of our country, and I've been humbled by the faith they've placed in me. I pledge to be a better man tomorrow, and will never, ever let you down."*

Then Trump tried to take attention off of what he said in the *Access Hollywood* recording by telling people he wanted to be honest by reminding them how terrible the world is. He said *"Let's be honest. We're living in the real world. This is nothing more than a distraction from the important issues we are facing today. We are losing our jobs, we are less safe than we were eight years ago and Washington is totally broken."*

Then Trump created a distraction to take attention off of his actions by claiming other people are worse than him. He said *"Hillary Clinton, and her kind, have run our country into the ground. I've said some foolish things, but there is a big difference between the words and actions of other people. Bill Clinton has actually abused women and Hillary has bullied, attacked, shamed and intimidated his victims. We will discuss this more in the coming days."*

Access Hollywood Scandal (5,6)
www.BluntHonest.com/Scandal

Trump Regrets Things He Said

After Trump became president, he seemed to regret apologizing for the *Access Hollywood* recording. *The New York Times* reported that Trump was telling people the recording was not an authentic.

Trump Is Delighted by the #MeToo Movement

Donald Trump was delighted by the #MeToo movement. He said *"Women are very special. I think it's a very special time because a lot of things are coming out, and I think that's good for our society, and I think it's very, very good for women. And I'm very happy a lot of these things are coming out, and I'm very happy it's being exposed."*

Trump Responds to Innuendos

Senator Kristen Gillibrand talked about the sexual misconduct allegations against Trump and said *"These allegations are credible. They are numerous. I've heard these women's testimony, and many of them are heartbreaking, and President Trump should resign his position."*

In response, Trump tweeted *"Lightweight Senator Kirsten Gillibrand, a total flunky for Chuck Schumer and someone who would come to my office "begging" for campaign contributions not so long ago (and would do anything for them), is now in the ring fighting against Trump. Very disloyal to Bill & Crooked-USED!"* – Dec 12, 2017

Trump Encourages Women to Celebrate

In January, 2018, as women around the nation gathered to protest the Trump administration, Trump tweeted *"Beautiful weather all over our great country, a perfect day for all Women to March. Get out there now to celebrate the historic milestones and unprecedented economic success and wealth creation that has taken place over the last 12 months. Lowest female unemployment in 18 years!"*

Trump Is Concerned by the #MeToo Movement

Two men from the White House staff resigned after women accused them of physical abuse. Trump expressed concern in a tweet saying *"Peoples lives are being shattered and destroyed by a mere allegation. Some are true and some are false. Some are old and some are new. There is no recovery for someone falsely accused - life and career are gone. Is there no such thing any longer as Due Process?"* – Feb 10, 2018

Trump stated some valid concerns in his tweet. However, perhaps those words would have been better received if they were sent by a different messenger. Trump has been accused by numerous women of sexual misconduct. He also seems to make unproven allegations.

Trump Encourages Oprah Winfrey to Run for President

On *60 Minutes*, Oprah Winfrey asked people if President Trump was being held to a different standard for the 20 women who had accused him of sexual misconduct. Later, Trump tweeted *"Just watched a very insecure Oprah Winfrey, who at one point I knew very well, interview a panel of people on 60 Minutes. The questions were biased and slanted, the facts incorrect. Hope Oprah runs so she can be exposed and defeated just like all of the others!"*

Trump Gives a Pep Talk to Shooting Victim

Samantha Fuentes, a victim of a Florida school shooting, was called by Trump in her hospital room. According to Fuentes *"He said he heard that I was a big fan of his, and then he said, 'I'm a big fan of yours, too.'"* Fuentes added *"I'm pretty sure he made that up."* Then she said, *"Talking to the president, I've never been so unimpressed by a person in my life."* She also said that Trump *"...called the shooter a sick puppy and probably used the words 'oh boy' a solid 8 times. I can't say that I was consoled or helped...He didn't express any real empathy."*

Trump Responds to Pleas from Puerto Rico Hurricane Victims

After the mayor of San Juan (Carmen Yulín Cruz) said more help was needed to save the lives of victims of the hurricane in Puerto Rico, Donald Trump promptly tweeted *"The Mayor of San Juan, who was very complimentary only a few days ago, has now been told by the Democrats that you must be nasty to Trump. Such poor leadership ability by the Mayor of San Juan, and others in Puerto Rico, who are not able to get their workers to help. They want everything to be done for them when it should be a community effort. 10,000 Federal workers now on Island doing a fantastic job."*

Trump Understands the Struggles of People with Disabilities

Donald Trump brought attention to how difficult it is for someone with a disability. In particular, he showed how it must feel to be mocked and ridiculed by a bully as he wowed his audience by his exaggerated contortions of his face and body as he slurred his speech to portray a reporter named Serge Kovaleski who has a disability.

Even though Trump did not receive any awards for his acting performance, one of the world's most renown actresses talked about how his performance moved her. Meryl Streep said that Donald's performance was *"one performance this year that stunned me."*

Trump Wants to Revitalize Water Sports

Donald Trump wants more participation in surfing, jet skiing, sailing, paddle boarding and other forms of outdoor recreation. In a 2016 presidential debate, Trump said *"I would bring back waterboarding, and I would bring back a hell of a lot worse than waterboarding."*

Trump Does Not Condone Violence

At a Trump rally in North Carolina, after a 78-year-old man punched a protester in the face, Trump said that he doesn't *"condone violence in any shape."*

Trump Offers to Pay Legal Expenses for an Elderly Man

At a Trump rally in North Carolina, a 78-year-old man was arrested for punching a protester in the face. Trump says he was looking into paying the costs of the man's legal defense.

Trump Says Middle Finger Gestures Are "Not Nice"

In North Carolina, after a 78-year-old man punched a protester in the face. Trump said the violence may have been the fault of the protestor who was taunting others. Trump said, *"There was a lot of taunting and a certain finger was placed in the air. Not nice."*

Trump Settles Things Amicably

USA Today reported that Trump and his businesses have been involved in at least 3,500 lawsuits and said his volume of lawsuits was *"unprecedented for a presidential nominee. No candidate of a major party has had anything approaching the number of Trump's courtroom entanglements."* In response, Trump tweeted *"Wow, USA Today did today's cover story on my record in lawsuits. Verdict: 450 wins, 38 losses. Isn't that what you want for your president?"*

Donald Trump Uses Sign Language

A spokesperson for the National Association of the Deaf said, *"It is refreshing to see Trump use sign language to communicate. Sometimes, people who cannot hear or read lips feel left out of politics. By using sign language, Trump helps them understand the debates."*

The spokesperson went on to say *"Sometimes his messages are confusing or gibberish, but other times the signs he makes are clear. For example, one of the signs that Trump most frequently uses is made by placing the pointer finger and thumb together to form a circle and extending the other three fingers outward. That sign means 'asshole.'"*

Trump Feels Bloody Entertainment Hurts Children

Comedian Kathy Griffin made a video holding a Trump mask that was covered in ketchup. In response, Donald Trump reminded the nation how violent entertainment affects children when he tweeted *"Kathy Griffin should be ashamed of herself. My children, especially my 11 year old son, Barron, are having a hard time with this. Sick!"*

Ironically, Trump's own description of bloody faces is what had inspired Kathy Griffin to create her video of ketchup on a mask. Trump had recently described Megyn Kelly as a woman who had *"blood coming out of her eyes, blood coming out of her wherever."*

Trump Prevents a Slaughter

Trump saved the lives of two turkeys at Thanksgiving time. At the pardoning ceremony he said *"Over the past 10 months, Melania and I have had the pleasure of welcoming many, many special visitors to the great White House. We've hosted dozens of incredible world leaders, members of Congress, and, along the way, a few very strange birds. But we have yet to receive any visitors quite like our magnificent guest of honor today... Drumstick, you are hereby pardoned. Drumstick and his friend Wishbone will live out their days at Gobbler's Rest. There they'll join Tator and Tot, the two turkeys pardoned last year by President Obama."*

Trump Polls the Nation and Listens

Trump asked the nation to decide which turkey would be pardoned for Thanksgiving and which turkey would be put to death. He announced a poll in a tweet *"Which turkey should be pardoned during the National Thanksgiving Turkey Pardoning Ceremony?"*

When the day of reckoning arrived, the turkeys spent the night with luxurious accommodations at the Willard Intercontinental Hotel. Normally it costs $3,500 a night to stay there. However, the turkeys did not have access to Twitter, so they probably didn't enjoy their night at the hotel as they worried about what was going to happen the next day.

On the day of judgment, 40,910 people had voted and 60 percent of poll results were in favor of pardoning Drumstick. Only 40 percent voted for Wishbone. Some people were concerned that Trump might not honor the wishes of the nation because Trump does not like dark meat. The nation feared he might claim the voting was rigged.

Trump accepted the poll results and pardoned Drumstick. He didn't pardon Wishbone but promised that Wishbone would live in peace. Rumor has it that Wishbone was not born in the United States and some people are concerned that Trump might use Wishbone's life as a pawn to force Congress to go along with Trump's plan to build a Mexican wall.

Trump Honors Obama's Decision

Trump promised he would not slaughter Obama's turkeys. He said, *"As many of you know I have been very active in overturning a number of executive actions of my predecessor...However, I have been informed by the White House counsel's office that Tater and Tot's pardons cannot, under any circumstances, be revoked— so, Tater and Tot, you can rest easy."*

Trump Pardons Joe Arpaio

Joe Arpaio was an Arizona sheriff who was held in criminal contempt for violating a court order to stop racial profiling tactics that targeted and detained Latinos. A White House statement said he was pardoned because *"Throughout his time as sheriff, Arpaio continued his life's work of protecting the public from the scourges of crime and illegal immigration."*

Trump Supports Roy Moore

When Roy Moore ran for Senate in Alabama, several women said he had pursued relationships with them as underage girls in the past. Trump supported Roy Moore's election campaign and he explained why in a tweet, *"Democrats refusal to give even one vote for massive Tax Cuts is why we need Republican Roy Moore to win in Alabama."*

Trump Leads a National Prayer

The National Prayer Breakfast is a solemn event attended by religious leaders. At the breakfast, Trump talked about how the *Apprentice* show ratings were affected after Arnold Schwarzenegger became the host. Trump said *"The ratings went right down the tubes. It has been a disaster...I want to just pray for Arnold ... for those ratings."*

Trump Warns of Potential Assassination Attempt

At a Trump election rally in Wilmington N.C, Trump warned Hillary Clinton that people might take matters into their own hands and use their second amendment rights (the ability to own guns). He said *"Hillary wants to abolish, essentially abolish, the Second Amendment. By the way, and if she gets to pick – if she gets to pick her judges, nothing you can do, folks. Although the Second Amendment people, maybe there is, I don't know. But I'll tell you what, that will be a horrible day, if – if – Hillary gets to put her judges in."*

Trump Gives Trophies to Hunters

The Trump administration announced it was ending Obama–era hunting bans. The changes allow hunters to bring the trophy heads of big game animals they killed, such as elephants, back into the U.S. Most hunters kill to get the trophy heads of the animals.

Some people believe the ban may have been ended because Trump's sons like to hunt elephants. Also, Trump appointed an International Wildlife Conservation Council that made the recommendation, and most of the members of the council are hunters.

Trump Saves the Elephants

After a public outcry over the removal of hunting restrictions on trophy hunters, Trump reinstated the hunting restrictions.

Trump Administration Pardons Bird Killers

The Trump administration reduced enforcement of the Migratory Bird Treaty Act (MBTA). This means industries no longer need to take precautions to avoid killing birds. The Audubon Society said the MBTA *"is one of the most important conservation laws we have."*

Trump Humanizes American Symbols

Donald Trump was personally involved with redesigning the presidential challenge coin. Challenge coins are given out by presidents to special guests, diplomats, and members of the military. In the past, one side of the coin had the presidential seal with a left-facing eagle and the Latin phrase "E pluribus unum," which means "Out of many, one." The other side of the coin had tastefully depicted the White House with a small flag shown on top of it and the name of the president was printed once on the coin. Past coins were copper or silver.

Trump's new coin pays homage to himself. His name appears on the coin four times. The presidential seal was replaced by a flamboyant right-facing eagle. The Latin words are gone. His slogan "Make America Great Again" is on both sides of the coin. The small flag on the white house has been replaced with a large colorful flag. His coin is larger and thicker than past presidential coins and is gold and shaped to look like an award ribbon.

Next, Trump plans to redesign the American flag and replace most of the stars with iconic images of himself. After the flag is redesigned, there will be little room left on it for stripes.

"Trump" Becomes a Synonym of "Integrity"

Trump displays a family crest at his properties in the USA and sells merchandise based on that crest. To create his crest, he plagiarized another family's crest. The original crest had the word "Integritas" on it which means "Integrity" and he replaced that word with "Trump." His plagiarism violates the Lyon King of Arms Act that was passed in 1672 to protect heraldry.

Trump Walks Away from His Bruised Ego

Trump claimed he was defamed by the author of *TrumpNation* and sued the author for $5 billion in damages. The book said Trump's net worth was only around $150 million to $250 million instead of the billions that Trump claimed to be worth. A judge threw out the lawsuit.

Trump Earns a Spot on the Forbes 400 List

The Washington Post reported that in 1984, a man named "John Barron" convinced Jonathan Greenberg, a reporter for *Forbes*, to put Donald Trump onto *Forbe's* annual list of America's richest people. Barron told Greenberg that Trump's assets were $400 million and that Trump would soon be a billionaire based upon all the success he was having. However, later research showed that Trump was probably worth around $5 million at that time, which was far too low to be in the *Forbes 400* list.

Later, it became known that "John Barron" was an alias name Trump used for himself. Greenberg said *"This was a model Trump would use for the rest of his career, telling a lie so cosmic that people believed that some kernel of it had to be real. The tactic landed him a place he hadn't earned on the Forbes list — and led to future accolades, press coverage and deals. It eventually paved a path toward the presidency."*

Trump Is the Healthiest President

In December, 2015, Trump's campaign released a letter from Dr. Harold Bornstein that said *"His physical strength and stamina are extraordinary...If elected, Mr. Trump, I can state unequivocally, will be the healthiest individual ever elected to the presidency."* In 2018, Bornstein told CNN that Trump *"dictated that whole letter. I didn't write that letter."*

Trump Honors the News Media with Awards

In late 2017, Trump tweeted *"We should have a contest as to which of the Networks, plus CNN and not including Fox, is the most dishonest, corrupt and/or distorted in its political coverage of your favorite President (me). They are all bad. Winner to receive the FAKE NEWS TROPHY!"* In January, 2018, Trump announced the winners of his "fake news" awards.

Trump gave a "Fake News" award to *Newsweek* for misreporting his handshake with the Polish First Lady. However, he failed to give honorable mentions to *Vanity Fair, Time*, or T*he Hill* for also incorrectly describing his handshake with her. Probably the most important fake news award went to *Newsweek* for incorrectly reporting that Trump overfed some Koi Fish.

There was no red–carpet award ceremony and no trophies were given to these organizations. They will just have to be satisfied by the dishonor bestowed upon their reputation that will follow them around forever online, or until some crazy–narcissistic leader has a temper tantrum and destroys the world by launching nuclear bombs.

Also, some people have said Trump is going to create "Fake Book" awards for books he doesn't like. Personally, I was hoping my book would win a Pulitzer Prize, a National Book Award, a Peabody Award, or perhaps the Nobel Peace Prize; I wouldn't even begin to hope for an award and recognition from Donald Trump.

In March, 2018, Monmouth University took a poll to measure what news sources people trust and compared that trust to their level of trust in the President. In all cases, people trusted news organizations more than they trusted Donald Trump. According to the poll, *CNN* was considered the most trustworthy news source and *Fox News* was least trustworthy.

Trump Wants to Eliminate Fake News

On May 9, 2018, Trump tweeted *"...91% of the Network News about me is negative (Fake). Why do we work so hard in working with the media when it is corrupt? Take away credentials?"* Trump seems to say that "fake news" means any negative stories about him and that he wants to control the news media. Trump later announced he wanted to double the US postal rates paid by Amazon. Amazon founder, Jeff Bezos, owns the *Washington Post* and sometimes the *Washington Post* prints negative stories about Trump.

National Enquirer Protects Reputations

The *National Enquirer* paid $150,000 to former Playboy model Karen McDougal to buy her story about the nine months she spent with Donald Trump starting in 2006. The agreement gave the *Enquirer "exclusive ownership of her account of any romantic, personal, or physical relationship she has ever had with any 'then-married man.'"*

Buying a story and not printing it is known in the industry as "catch and kill." It prevents a person from selling their story to someone else. Tabloids like to "know where the bodies are buried" because they can use unpublished stories to blackmail people for favors.

In this situation, the story may have been silenced as a favor for Trump. Davide Pecker, publisher of the *National Enquirer*, is friends with Trump.

Trump Compliments the National Enquirer

Trump said, *"Why didn't the National Enquirer get the Pulitzer Prize for Edwards? They actually have a very good record of being right."*

Trump's Military Experiences

Trump said his love life has made him *"a great and very brave soldier."* At times, his personal life seems to be an example of the military acronyms SNAFU and FUBAR.

National Enquirer Solves JFK Assassination, Elvis Mystery, Hoffa Burial

The *National Enquirer* released a photograph it claimed showed Ted Cruz's father and Lee Harvey Oswald together. The photo was taken several months before Oswald assassinated John F. Kennedy.

During the presidential campaign, Trump used that story to create a conspiracy theory about Cruz's father. Trump said *"What was he doing with Lee Harvey Oswald shortly before the death, I mean, before the shooting? It's horrible."*

Trump assumed that the person in the photo actually was Ted Cruz's father. He assumed the photo proved that Ted Cruz's father actually had a close relationship with Oswald. Also, Trump insinuates that Cruz's father's reputation affects Ted Cruz's reputation.

In response to Trump's conspiracy theories, Ted Cruz mocked Trump and said *"Yes, my dad killed JFK, he is secretly Elvis, and Jimmy Hoffa is buried in his backyard."* Some people have said that Trump wanted authorities to excavate the backyard of Cruz's father to look for Hoffa's grave.

Trump Releases JFK Assassination Records

In October, 2017, the Trump administration complied with a law passed in 1992 that mandated that the JFK assassination records needed to be released. Over 2,800 confidential JFK records were released to the public, but the Trump White House kept 300 files classified, saying they contained information of concern to national security.

An anonymous source, who works in the White House, said that Trump was concerned those documents may prove that Ted Cruz's father had nothing to do with the assassination of JFK. Donald Trump has never been wrong before and anything that made him look like he is an idiot might be a distraction from his ability to mismanage the country as President.

PLAYMATE KAREN   PORNSTAR STORMY

Trump Gives Credit to CNN for Representing USA to the World

In November, 2017, Donald Trump notified the world that *CNN* is responsible for the reputation of the United States. He tweeted *"Fox News is MUCH more important in the United States than CNN, but outside of the U.S., CNN International is still a major source of (Fake) news, and they represent our Nation to the WORLD very poorly. The outside world does not see the truth from them!"*

Soon after the President's tweet, *CNN* responded by saying *"It's not CNN's job to represent the U.S to the world. That's yours. Our job is to report the news."*

After Trump said *CNN* creates "fake news," people around the world were relieved that they didn't have to take *CNN* seriously. For example, around the time Trump told people that *CNN* was a source of "fake news," *CNN* released a story about slave auctions in Libya. Libyan officials and Libyan news media used Trump's claims that *CNN* creates fake news to question the legitimacy of the Libya slave trade story.

Some journalists began to worry more about their safety. At times the news media can be a dangerous profession, but to have the President of the United States telling the world not to trust news organizations may put journalists in even more harm's way.

In response to Trump's tweet, A CNN reporter, Christiane Amanpour, shared a picture of a late colleague and tweeted *"If President Trump knew the facts he would never have sent that tweet. Here is my (late) camerawoman Margaret Moth, who took a bullet in the face covering the facts and truth in Bosnia. #FactsFirst."*

Trump Is Not Interested in Being 'Man of the Year'

In November, 2017 Trump tweeted *"Time Magazine called to say that I was PROBABLY going to be named "Man (Person) of the Year," like last year, but I would have to agree to an interview and a major photo shoot. I said probably is no good and took a pass. Thanks anyway!"*

In response, *Time Magazine* tweeted *"The President is incorrect about how we choose Person of the Year. TIME does not comment on our choice until publication, which is December 6."*

Trump Is Humbled by His Time Magazine World Record

Trump claimed he was on the cover of *Time* magazine more often than anyone else. However, that seems to be fake news. Richard Nixon actually appeared the most times on the magazine's cover. Perhaps Trump was including all the fake pictures of himself on the cover of *Time* magazine. *Time* magazine asked him to remove those fake cover pictures that were hanging up at his golf resorts.

Trump Explains the Role of "Fake News"

The journalist Leslie Stahl asked Trump why he kept accusing the news media of "fake news." She said Trump told her *"I do it to discredit you all and demean you all so that when you write negative stories about me no one will believe you."*

Trump Avoids Conflict of Interest

Donald Trump creates a lot of fake news, but he is not eligible for a Fake News award because he is the judge of the awards. However, if someone created an award for the most screwed up idiot, Trump would likely win.

Trump Appreciates Fine Art

Trump's biographer, Tim O'Brien, said Trump showed him the famous Renoir painting "Two Sisters (On the Terrace)" hanging up in his apartment and Trump claimed it is the original. However, the Art Institute of Chicago says that they have the original painting in their museum, and 1.5 million people see it each year. The Art Institute of Chicago says it is "satisfied our version is real." Every art expert who has weighed in on the matter agrees.

Trump Cares About Irreplaceable Historic Monuments

Trump is a big fan of confederate statues and things that remind people of the heritage that the United States was founded on. He said *"Sad to see the history and culture of our great country being ripped apart with the removal of our beautiful statues and monuments. You... can't change history, but you can learn from it. Robert E Lee, Stonewall Jackson - who's next, Washington, Jefferson? So foolish! Also... the beauty that is being taken out of our cities, towns and parks will be greatly missed and never able to be comparably replaced!"*

It seems Trump has had a change of heart because in 2016 he scrapped the historic parts of the Washington DC post office to turn it into a Trump Hotel. That building was constructed in 1899 in a stunning Romanesque Revival style. John Cullinane, the preservationist architect working on that project, resigned because he *"couldn't support what they were doing to the building...they were covering up or tearing out everything that was historic."*

Trump Promises to Donate Art to the Metropolitan Museum of Art

Many people considered the Bonwit Teller department store to be a historic landmark. The store was built in 1895, but it was not officially protected as a landmark. Donald Trump bought the building in 1979 to demolish it and make way for Trump Tower. This caused people to become concerned about the loss of the beautiful architecture of the historic building.

To alleviate people's concerns, Trump promised to remove two large limestone Art Deco sculptures and metal grillwork from the building and donate them to the Metropolitan Museum of Art to be preserved and enjoyed for current and future generations.

Art expert Robert Miller said they were extraordinary works of art by Beaux-Arts designers Whitney Warren and Charles Wetmore. Miller appraised their value to be worth "several hundred thousand dollars" and said, *"The reliefs are as important as the sculptures on the Rockefeller building. They'll never be made again."*

Later, Trump reneged on his promise to donate the sculptures to the Metropolitan so that he could avoid delaying his project. His workmen used jackhammers to pulverize the art before he tore down the building.

After Trump destroyed the precious art, there was a public outcry and Trump went into hiding. All correspondence to deal with the public relations mess was handled by his Vice President, John Barron, who helped to sooth the outraged public. He justified what Trump had done by telling the public that the value of the destroyed art was only $9,000 and it would have cost $32,000 to remove the art, and the delays to the construction time would have cost the developer $500,000.

Years later, after John Barron had stepped in to solve numerous public relations problems for Trump, it was determined that John Barron was just a made-up pseudo name for Trump. John Barron was actually Trump defending himself under another name. It seems the $9,000 valuation of the art was greatly minimized by Trump and so perhaps the $500,000 cost was greatly exaggerated by him to justify not honoring his promise to the Metropolitan.

In 1998, 18 years after the demolition work was done, Trump finally paid $1.4 million to settle a lawsuit for employing undocumented Polish workers to demolish the store.

Trump Helps Foreign Workers

Trump says he wants to put America first and put Americans back to work. When Jimmy Kimmel ordered Trump-branded products from the Trump Organization's website, many of those products were made in China, Thailand, and Peru. When Trump put tariffs on Chinese products coming into the United States, he avoided putting any tariffs on clothing. Tariffs would hurt his daughter's business, a company that makes clothing in China.

Mexico Will Pay for Trump's Wall

Trump has put a tariff on all Mexican restaurants in the United States to pay for the wall.

Trump Creates a Sacred Historical War Monument

In 2009, while renovating his Sterling Virginia golf course, Trump installed a stone pedestal to commemorate historic sacrifices made by soldiers during the Civil War. According to Trump, so many people died at the location of his golf course, that the river turned red from the loss of life and that area became known as "The River of Blood."

The pedestal says *"Many great American soldiers, both of the North and South, died at this spot, "The Rapids," on the Potomac River. The casualties were so great that the water would turn red and thus became known as "The River of Blood."* The plaque also has Trump's name and Trump's plagiarized family crest and says *"It is my great honor to have preserved this important section of the Potomac River!"*

However, historians say that there never was a Civil War battle at the location of his golf course. Trump responded that he checked with "many historians." Trump refused to name his historians and went on to say *"That was a prime site for river crossings...So, if people are crossing the river, and you happen to be in a civil war, I would say that people were shot — a lot of them."* As more historians began to criticize the accuracy of Trump's monument, Trump criticized the historians and said *"How would they know that? Were they there?"*

Great Energy Permeates the White House as Trump Seeks Perfection

During his first year in office there was a 34% turnover in Trump's administration. The three previous administrations – Obama, Bush, and Clinton – had much lower first year turn-overs — 9%, 6%, and 11%, respectively. The exodus of his staff increased in March, 2018. When the news media reported there was chaos in the White House, Trump tweeted: *"The new Fake News narrative is that there is CHAOS in the White House. Wrong! People will always come & go, and I want strong dialogue before making a final decision. I still have some people that I want to change (always seeking perfection). There is no Chaos, only great Energy!"*

Trump May Receive a Nobel Prize

Trump is being considered for a Nobel Prize for his contributions to chaos theory.

Trump Admires Barack Obama

In 2012, Trump tweeted *"President @BarackObama's vacation is costing taxpayers millions of dollars----Unbelievable!"* In 2014, Trump tweeted *"Can you believe that, with all of the problems and difficulties facing the U.S., President Obama spent the day playing golf."*

Trump Holds Himself to Higher Standards

During his first year in office, Trump went golfing 95 times and spent 117 days visiting Trump properties. During Barack Obama's first year in office, Obama only golfed 26 times.

Trump Is an Expert at Time Management

Trump told *The Hill* in 2015 *"I would rarely leave the White House because there's so much work to be done...I would not be a president who took vacations. I would not be a president that takes time off."* While campaigning in 2016, Trump said *"I'm going to be working for you. I'm not going to have time to go play golf."* Now that he is in office, Trump has found plenty of time to golf and travel.

Trump Remained Calm During Missile Warning

On January 13, 2018, cell phones and news media throughout Hawaii received a text message saying "BALLISTIC MISSILE THREAT INBOUND TO HAWAII. SEEK IMMEDIATE SHELTER. THIS IS NOT A DRILL." A few weeks earlier, Trump had bickered with the leader of North Korea and people were concerned that North Korea might launch nuclear weapons.

Unknown to the panicked residents of Hawaii, a government employee had pressed the wrong button and sent that warning by mistake. It took 30 minutes for people to learn they were safe. During that time of uncertainty, many reached out to loved ones to say goodbye.

Donald Trump was golfing that day when the false missile warning occurred. He continued to play golf during the crisis. Four hours after the false missile warning, Trump sent out his first tweet for that day. He tweeted *"So much Fake News is being reported. They don't even try to get it right, or correct it when they are wrong. They promote the Fake Book of a mentally deranged author, who knowingly writes false information. The Mainstream Media is crazed that WE won the election!"*

Trump Loves Babies

Trump was giving a speech in Ashburn, Virginia when a baby started crying in the audience. He said: *"Don't worry about that baby. I love babies. I love babies. I hear that baby crying, I like it. I like it. What a baby. What a beautiful baby. Don't worry, don't worry. The mom's running around. Don't worry about it. It's young, and healthy, and beautiful, and that's what we want...Actually, I was only kidding. You can get that baby out of here. That's all right don't worry. I think she really believed me that I loved having a baby crying while I'm speaking."*

Stranger Shows Concern for a Little Girl

On the television show *60 Minutes*, porn star Stormy Daniels talked about how a stranger gave her some advice in 2011 to encourage her to avoid talking about her alleged affair with Donald Trump. Daniels said *"I was in a parking lot, going to a fitness class with my infant daughter...and a guy walked up on me and said to me, 'Leave Trump alone. Forget the story.' And then he leaned around and looked at my daughter and said, 'That's a beautiful little girl. It'd be a shame if something happened to her mom.'"*

Trump "Drains the Swamp"

Trump promised to "drain the swamp" and he is now building moats to protect the castles and fortunes of wealthy people. Several billionaires are on his advisory boards. He has given tax breaks to the wealthy and rolled back regulations on pollution to let companies profit from harming the environment.

Unfit News

You have reached the end of the fake news section of this book. When Blunt Honest is not out saving the world, he is a mild-mannered reporter for *Unfit News,* an organization that covers all the news that is unfit to print. *Unfit News,* is the world's leading source of "fake news." We pride ourselves on taking real news stories and putting a positive spin on them.

Most news organizations look for scandals to sensationalize the problems of the world. Our news organization is much different. We look for silver linings in everything. We'll make idiots seem like geniuses and we will turn tragedies into triumphs. We want the world to be a happier place full of generous, loving, kind, creative, intelligent people who are nice to each other. To learn more, visit:

www.UnfitNews.com

What Trump Knows About Empathy

Many people think that Donald Trump, based on how he treats people, doesn't know anything about empathy. Moments that call for Donald Trump to rise above himself, to be a leader, and to help show the way, are moments that are met with a profound lack of empathy. However, even though Trump lacks empathy, he actually knows a lot about empathy. In particular, he knows how to influence and take advantage of the empathy of others.

Trump often portrays himself as a victim. For example, he claims to be a victim of the "fake news" media. He said Obama wiretapped him. He says the Russian investigation is a "witch hunt." When Trump portrays himself as a victim, he is appealing to the empathy of others to convince them to support him and rally against his "unfair" opponents.

The President of the United States Cordially Invites You to A Pity Party

Trump also calls people, or groups of people, names. For example, he calls people "crooked" or "rapists" or "terrorists." By dehumanizing others, he can influence his followers to suppress or reduce their empathy for the people or groups he targets. When others lower their levels of empathy, they are less likely to speak out when actions are taken against the people being dehumanized.

Trump can be very critical of others, and he often uses tactics involving shame and guilt. By attempting to embarrass or humiliate others, he is trying to manipulate the conscience of the people he targets. Trump resorts to bullying tactics such as publicly blaming and shaming people to control and manipulate them. A person who is shamed or blamed by a bully may lose self-esteem and self-worth, even if that person has done nothing wrong. These tactics serve to weaken his opponents both internally and externally by reducing their credibility with others.

There are times Trump has given money to people. Those acts of charity may seem like empathy, but he tends to brag about and exaggerate his charitable work. This makes it seem as though his charitable actions are mainly done for self-promotion rather than to help someone else. There have been concerns about how some money donated to his charitable foundation has been used to pay for personal items for Trump (such as an expensive portrait) or that charitable funds have been spent on business interests he has.

At times, Trump tries to say the right things to look as though he has empathy, but often his words are hollow because his actions don't correspond to his words. He tells others what they should do but doesn't follow his own advice. There have been occasions he has claimed to help someone and then he later criticizes them because they did not praise or thank him enough.

The next several chapters show how abusive tactics can be used to control or influence people's empathy. We'll also look at how empathy and narcissism affect the world.

Stockholm Syndrome

Donald Trump seems to compliment a person one day, and soon after he criticizes them. One moment he is their friend, the next moment he wants nothing to do with them, then they are friends again. His inconsistent behavior can be a powerful form of motivation known as intermittent reinforcement.

Intermittent reinforcement can be a form of abuse that causes trauma bonding in the person who is being abused. The victim may come to feel loyal and supportive towards the person who has abused them. Trauma bonding is also known as the Stockholm Syndrome. This syndrome was named after a famous bank robbery.

In 1973, a man with a gun entered a bank in Stockholm, Sweden and announced: *"The party has just begun."* The police surrounded the bank and a standoff occurred. Four bank employees were held hostage for five days.

The gunman strapped dynamite to the hostages and held them captive in a bank vault. He also threatened to hang them from a noose. The hostages got to know their captor and began to express sympathy for him. The victims emotionally bonded with their abuser and this phenomenon became known as the Stockholm Syndrome.

Emotional bonds formed by trauma can cause irrational decisions. In particular, a victim of trauma bonding might stand up for and support their abuser or even fall in love with their abuser. Perhaps some of Trump's closest supporters have been affected by the Stockholm Syndrome.

Boiling Frogs

There is an allegory that describes a frog being boiled alive. If a frog were put into a boiling hot pot of water, it would quickly realize it was in danger and jump out of the pot. However, if a frog is put into water that is at room temperature, the frog will feel comfortable and stay in the water. Then when the water temperature is gradually raised, the frog will not sense any danger because each small rise in temperature doesn't seem to be noticeable to the frog.

The frog gets used to the temperature of the water as it gradually gets hotter. Eventually, the frog gets boiled alive and doesn't see the danger he is in until it is too late.

Relationships with abusive personalities tend to start out like a normal relationship and then craziness and abuse gradually escalates over time. A narcissist may test the waters to see how far they can push things with their victim. Over time, a victim becomes used to one level of abuse, and this makes it easier for them to accept a slightly greater level of abuse. Eventually, a victim may find themselves in an extremely abusive situation but the abuse may not feel so bad because the level of abuse increased slowly over time.

The boiling frog principle can also affect large groups of people. A leader might start out making lots of promises; the leader may appear to be charismatic and appealing to the needs and desires of the people they govern. But then, over time, the leader may take away the rights of some citizens and become more controlling or dishonest.

When a leader gradually changes the rules of acceptable behavior, a "new-normal" may take place, and acting crazy and absurd starts to feel normal, as the bar of what is acceptable behavior becomes gradually lowered over time. For example, a leader who becomes known for misbehaving might be praised for doing what used to be normal and expected behavior.

The Emperor Has No Clothes

Some people seem to accept or support Trump because it is easier to tolerate him than to deal with the criticism and drama that results from disagreeing with him. Enabling someone to be controlling, abusive, or dishonest is an indirect form of supporting them. People who appear to support or go along with Trump are enabling his misconduct.

Sometimes people fail to see problems because of cognitive dissonance. Cognitive dissonance is an unwillingness to face the facts that are contrary to beliefs we've already formed. Cognitive dissonance can cause an uncomfortable feeling as people struggle to find ways to make the facts fit their false beliefs. Rather than change their beliefs, people may find ways to justify their false beliefs and ignore the facts.

What Is Empathy?

In 1914, during World War I, German and British soldiers were hiding in trenches and trying to kill each other. But as Christmas approached, they began to sing songs. Then the soldiers crawled out of their trenches and met each other. They shook hands and played football. They shared food and gifts and even fell asleep next to each other. They exchanged mailing addresses and promised to contact each other after the war. What allowed these enemies to suddenly lay down their arms and befriend each other? Perhaps it was empathy.

Empathy lets you put yourself into another's situation and understand how they feel. You don't want to hurt them, because hurting them will feel like hurting yourself. Empathy helps people trust others. It creates cooperation and mutual respect. Empathy is the foundation of love, sympathy, and compassion.

Types of Empathy

Most people experience three main types of empathy: reflexive empathy, emotional empathy, and cognitive empathy. Some people experience a fourth type known as compassionate empathy. There is also a rare fifth type of empathy known as mirror-touch synesthesia.

People seem to be born with reflexive empathy. It causes people to automatically react to the emotions of others. For example, if a baby cries, other babies nearby may also cry. If someone laughs, other people may start laughing. Reflexive empathy may be caused by mirror neurons in the brain.

Emotional empathy involves feeling the emotions of someone else. If someone feels hurt, emotional empathy may cause you to feel their hurt. If they feel joy, you may feel their joy.

Cognitive empathy helps you determine how a person feels based on things such as reading their emotions and body language. Cognitive empathy helps you predict what someone else may think or feel. It can help you understand their perspective and help you to motivate or negotiate with them. Cognitive empathy helps you understand how someone feels; emotional empathy helps you feel how they feel.

Compassionate empathy can cause a strong desire to help someone who is in need. Some people will risk their life to save a stranger while others will not. Some people will give a kidney to a stranger. Many people have compassionate empathy for people they love and may lack compassionate empathy for strangers.

A fifth type of empathy is mirror-touch synesthesia. This condition affects two percent of people and it lets them experience the physical sensations they observe someone else having. For example, they may feel pain in their finger when they see another person cut their finger.

Most people have the three main types of empathy, but some people only have one or two of the main kinds of empathy. Some people have greater amounts of empathy than others. People with strong empathy are sometimes called empaths. People who lack empathy are often called narcissists.

Warm Empathy and Cold Empathy

A person may have warm empathy or cold empathy. Warm empathy is when they feel the emotions of someone else. Cold empathy is when they are aware of how someone else feels but they don't feel the others' emotions. Most people experience both warm and cold empathy. For example, a person may have warm empathy for people who belong to their religion and cold empathy towards people of other religions. You may have warm empathy for your family and cold empathy towards a homeless person.

Pity can be a form of cold empathy. When you pity someone, you might observe them and feel discomfort for their situation but you don't really feel like they feel. Warm empathy feels more like you personally identify with the feelings of someone else.

Emotional empathy plays a role in experiencing warm or cold empathy. In general, we don't feel emotional empathy for most objects, but there are times we may feel emotional attachments to some objects, such as a family heirloom. Someone who hoards objects may feel greater levels of emotional attachments towards objects. When we lack emotional empathy for living beings, then we might treat living beings as though they are objects.

For example, a person may have warm empathy for cats and dogs, and cold empathy towards cows and pigs. If a cat or dog was confined and slaughtered, the person who felt indifferent (cold empathy) for farm animals, might have strong feelings (warm empathy) when a cat or dog is treated like a farm animal. People may be aware of the pain and suffering caused to farm animals but find ways to justify suppressing their empathy for farm animals, so that they can consume meat or animal products and not feel guilt for how their actions harm these animals.

Empathy and Conscience

Empathy affects your conscience. Cartoons sometimes represent the conscience as being a devil on one shoulder and an angel on the other shoulder. The devil tells us to do what is best for ourselves. The angel tells us to think about others. The devil expresses empathy for ourselves and the angel offers empathy to others.

The combination of an angel and devil helps us balance our needs and wants with the needs and wants of others. We need both an angel and a devil guiding us. Codependents tend to suppress their devil part and their angel part tries too hard to please others. Our devil part can help us set healthy boundaries. When we ignore the devil part of our conscience, sometimes we allow our inner child to get hurt and then we feel angry at ourselves.

People who lack empathy for others are like people who have a devil on their shoulder, but they are missing an angel. When no angel is offering guidance, they don't experience shame and guilt and they may have less self-control.

The angel part helps us feel good when we do things for others. A person who lacks empathy may not get a good feeling when helping others. People who lack empathy tend to be more selfish.

It is estimated that around one to four percent of humans may have empathy deficiencies. The most cruel and insensitive people tend to lack empathy. In the book *The Science of Evil,* (Simon Baron-Cohen, Basic Books, 2011) the author says in order to understand what makes somebody evil you need to understand a person's level of empathy. A lack of empathy appears to have a direct correlation to how evil a person may be.

Empathy Affects Intelligence and Perceptions

People often think of intelligence in terms of IQ (Intelligence Quotient) but there is another form of intelligence called EQ (Emotional Quotient). Emotional intelligence involves the ability to self-reflect, manage oneself, understand others, and have good relationships.

A lack of emotional empathy can reduce a person's EQ. Someone may have a high IQ and a low EQ or vice versa. A high IQ helps someone solve business or math problems. A high EQ helps someone with emotions and relationships. A high IQ is like being book smart and a high EQ is like being street smart.

If a person only has two of the main kinds of empathy, they might not realize this. Even if they learned about a type of empathy they lacked, it may be difficult for them to understand something they have not experienced. A person who lacks a form of empathy, may have difficulty understanding or relating to other people.

Empathy is like a guidance system that helps us interact with others. Think of how global positioning systems (GPS) work. For your smartphone to find a location, its GPS needs to receive signals from at least three satellites. If your GPS does not receive three good signals, then your device's navigation will not work very well.

Now let's consider how lacking a main type of empathy affects people. Narcissists tend to lack emotional empathy. However, a narcissist may have a high level of cognitive empathy. Sometimes narcissists are overly confident in their ability to read others and they act like they know more about what someone is thinking and feeling than the person whom they are observing. A narcissist might misuse their cognitive empathy to take advantage of others. A narcissist's lack of emotional empathy makes it easier for them to hurt others.

A person with autism may have lower levels of cognitive empathy. They may have difficulty reading people's body language or emotions. They may have high levels of emotional empathy, but their inability to read another person may make it more difficult for them to interpret and express empathy.

Empathy helps people to develop trust in others. When two people have empathy for each other it's like building a bridge and both sides want to develop a relationship to connect with each other. Sometimes people assume others are like themselves. For example, a person who is trustworthy may assume others are trustworthy. Someone who is dishonest may assume others are dishonest. What people think of their outer world is often a reflection of their inner world. How we perceive others and how we perceive our world is affected by our levels of empathy and the types of empathy we have.

Development of Empathy

Scientists believe that the anterior insular cortex part of the brain controls empathy. If that part of the brain is defective a person may not be able to develop, use, or retain empathy skills. A person may also lose empathy skills if they experience injuries to their brain. Empathy may also be affected by genetics. Some studies have indicated that certain gene expressions may be linked to more aggressive or anti-social behavior.

Much of a person's empathy skills are learned as a child. Young children tend to be narcissistic. Their whole world revolves around them. Around the age of four, children start to develop empathy skills. Parents are role models from whom children learn empathy.

Sometimes parents are too protective or too gloating. They put their kids on a pedestal and shield them from the difficulties of life. Some parents act like their child is always right and everything the child does is great. Some parents avoid saying or doing anything that may make their child uncomfortable. Empathy is often learned by talking about emotions and consequences of actions. This encourages self-reflection and growth. Sheltering someone from life lessons may reduce their ability to develop empathy skills.

Empathy is like a non-verbal language. Like most languages, it may be easier to learn empathy as a child than to learn it as an adult. If parents don't teach their children empathy, then they may lack empathy as an adult. However, there can be brain and genetic conditions that may make it difficult for a child to learn empathy skills even if they have great parents.

Animals also appear to experience empathy. Some animals show compassion for their mates, their offspring, or other animals. Animals also show empathy for animals of other species. Empathy has been observed in apes, elephants, dolphins, rats, and other animals.

Empathy seems to help animals live together in groups. "Survival of the fittest" is like a narcissistic trait for animals who must look out for themselves, but empathy is like "survival of the group" and it helps animals look out for the interests of the group. For animals that live in groups, selective breeding may reduce narcissistic traits in the population because animals who don't cooperate with the group may be ostracized by the group.

Sharing Empathy

People tend to feel more empathy for individuals than for groups. Psychologists call this the "identifiable victim affect." This affect can cause empathy to be disproportionate. We may be more willing to give attention and support to an individual, even though the needs of a group may be more serious than the needs of that individual.

People tend to think empathy is something exchanged between people who know each other, but empathy is more than that. You can show empathy by how you talk to someone online that you'll never meet. You can give empathy to someone who died by respecting their wishes. You can show empathy towards people who aren't born yet by how you treat this planet. You can show empathy for people who lived in the past by respecting historic artifacts.

You can share and receive empathy with other creatures. You may show empathy for an organization, a religion, or a place. In some cultures, things or animals may have "personhood" rights that are similar to the rights of a person. For example, a river may be considered to have "personhood" and may deserve to be treated with empathy and respect. It may seem odd to give empathy to a river, but when you consider the chain of life that may rely on a river, by giving empathy to a river you give empathy to the flow of life that relies on that river.

Empathy, or a lack of empathy, occurs in your thoughts, words, and actions. Empathy can ripple through time and affect the past, present, and future. Much of the difficulties we have in this world are related to a lack of empathy. War, prejudice, genocides, injustice, hatred, self-ishness, dishonesty, greed, and environmental harm are manifestations of a lack of empathy.

It would be easier to resolve our problems if human beings had broader and more consistent levels of empathy towards people, animals, and the Earth.

The Ultimate Golden Rule

In a way, empathy is like the golden rule. Many cultures and religions have a golden rule dealing with how to treat others. Sometimes this rule is called the "law of reciprocity." Often, the traditional golden rule is described as "Do unto others as you would have them do unto you."

Most people know about the golden rule and they think that they abide by it. However, there seems to be a flaw in how people sometimes interpret the wording of the traditional golden rule. Sometimes people treat others the way they want to be treated rather than how others want to be treated. When this happens, a profound lack of empathy and lack of respect may occur.

For example, some people project their sexuality or religious beliefs onto others and expect others to be like themselves. A Christian, heterosexual person may try to get another person to adopt their religion and their sexuality rather than respect and tolerate the religious beliefs and the orientation of that other person.

Perhaps we need to change how we think about the golden rule and consider an ultimate golden rule that says "Do unto others as they would have done unto themselves."

By following the ultimate golden rule, we would accept and respect others as they want to be and not try to change them. The ultimate golden rule also would not be limited to people. It would affect how we treat animals. If we did unto cows what cows would want to have done unto themselves, then we would treat cows differently.

The ultimate golden rule is not restricted by time. Often, we only think about the here and the now, and fail to consider how our actions cause repercussions in time that affect future generations. The ultimate golden rule would be to do unto future generations as they would want done unto themselves.

The Power of Empathy (9)
www.BluntHonest.com/Empathy

An Empathy Experiment

One day I was watching videos on YouTube that showed different children singing. I noticed that some of the children seemed to resonate more with me than others. I simply felt closer to some of the children.

At first, I thought it might be the song or that some songs were in languages I did not know. But then I found videos of other children singing the same song in English and in those videos some children still resonated more with me.

Then I thought perhaps some children were better singers or the video quality was better, but after looking closely I realized quality of singing or video quality didn't have much effect on which children resonated with me. I didn't know any of the children, yet I felt closer to some more than others.

After testing many variables, I realized the children that resonated with me the most were the ones who reminded me of myself when I was a child or they reminded me of my childhood. The children I felt most connected to were the ones I felt I could most identify with.

Perhaps a person's response to different kinds of children may be a good experiment involving empathy. Children are easy to like and trust. We were all children once so we have something in common. It is harder for us to trust and like adults who are strangers, and yet easier for us to trust and like children who are strangers.

Here is a video montage of children and young adults performing music. When you watch these videos, see if any performers resonate more with you and ask yourself why. Does their race or gender affect how they resonate with you? Does their religion or ethnicity affect how you feel towards them? For groups of people, do you recognize their differences or mainly see their similarities? How does your ability to see their differences affect how they resonate with you?

Young People Performing (7, 8)
www.BluntHonest.com/Sing

Problems with Empathy

Most people view empathy as being good and usually it is. However, sometimes empathy can be misguided or cause difficulties.

Sometimes, it is difficult to express empathy, especially when people are dealing with a tragedy. There are times when no words can help someone who is suffering. In these situations, perhaps the greatest way to show empathy is to be present and listen to the person who experienced a tragedy.

At times, too much empathy can make it difficult to make decisions or take necessary actions. For example, people who work in emergency situations may become overwhelmed if they feel too much empathy for the people they are helping. A doctor may have difficulty performing surgery on their spouse and another doctor may be able to focus better while performing the surgery.

Sometimes when you share empathy, you put yourself at risk. In these situations, it is important the other person has empathy for you. When you give empathy to someone who lacks empathy it's like petting a dog with rabies. Your trust can result in you being harmed.

Cognitive dissonance can affect when a person shares empathy. Cognitive dissonance is when a person feels a contradiction in their beliefs but finds a way to justify the contradiction. For example, a person should leave an abusive partner, but it makes them uncomfortable to realize their partner might not love them and so they find reasons to justify the abuse and stay with their partner. Sometimes people have too much empathy for someone who is harming them.

Empathy may cause us to misjudge a person. When a new acquaintance reminds us of someone who we love and trust, we might treat the acquaintance like we already know them and extend more empathy and trust to them. This can get us into trouble. First impressions can lead us astray. It takes time to see someone's true colors.

Predators may exploit empathy. For example, a child molester might ask a child to help them look for a lost puppy. A con artist might swindle money from someone who loves them.

Sometimes, our empathy causes us to assume others are like ourselves and we assume they share our motives and values. For example, if a person filed police charges against someone else, you might think "I'd only file police charges if someone harmed me." Then you may assume the person who was charged with a crime must have done something terrible to the person who claims to be a victim.

However, there are times false victims make up outrageous lies and use the police to harass others. In these situations, the real victim is the person who is falsely charged. Using your empathy and projecting yourself onto the person who claimed to be the victim can cause you to misinterpret the situation.

An abusive personality can misuse a person's empathy and use them to hurt others. An abuser might falsely portray themselves as being a victim and may encourage others to stand up for them. For example, let's say someone tells you they were harmed by an abusive person. Then your empathy compels you to warn others about that abusive person. But later you find out you were lied to. This makes you realize you were recruited by a liar to help them spread lies about another person.

People may unknowingly become abusers on behalf of a person who is lying. This is known as "proxy recruitment." In a proxy recruitment, the real victim is the person who the abuser has lied about and the recruits who harm the real victim are sometimes called "flying monkeys."

This term is from the *Wizard of Oz* movie. In the movie, a wicked witch (the abuser) took control of flying monkeys and used them to harass Dorothy (the real victim).

In extreme situations, we don't try to put ourselves in someone else's place. For example, Jeffrey Dahmer killed 17 men and boys. He dismembered and ate them. In a case like this, people are unlikely to try and put themselves in his shoes to understand him. We can't use empathy to try and understand the actions or motivations of someone who lacks empathy.

When a person lacks empathy, we need to avoid viewing their actions through an empathetic lens because that can cause us to misinterpret things. It can be difficult to tell if a person lacks empathy. Sometimes, people who lack empathy are good at faking human emotions and hiding behind a mask of sanity. It takes time to see a person's true colors.

Empathetic people tend to give others the benefit of the doubt. At times empathy is taken advantage of. For example, a dishonest person may tell a lie that is partially true or vague. If they are caught, they point out the true parts of their lie or use the vague parts to claim there was a misunderstanding. Liars create doubts to misuse our empathy so they can avoid being held accountable.

Abusive people can use empathy as a form of ransom. For example, in India, children are kidnapped by organized crime rings and forced to beg. Some captors blind the children, remove their limbs, or scar their faces with acid. They do this because severely disabled children can collect more money from empathetic tourists. The tourists don't realize that by giving money to the disfigured children they are encouraging their abusers to harm more children. The money goes to the abusive captors and the children are kept malnourished, because skeletal starving children collect more money from empathetic givers.

In Africa, a charity was paying slave traders to free their slaves. These payments encouraged slave traders to capture more slaves. In some cases, people volunteered to become "slaves" to share in the ransom paid by the charity. Instead of ending slavery, the charity was creating demand for the slave trade industry.

Empathy is often good, but we need to be careful who we give empathy to. When it comes to dishonest or abusive personalities, it may be wise to express less empathy for them.

Trump's View of the Universe

A Deadly Island

My college philosophy professor had students participate in an experiment that involved group empathy. He had us play a game called "The Rawls Game." It was based on the ideas of John Rawls.

First, the professor handed out colored coins. Most students received a red coin; a few students received a green coin. Then he told us to imagine we lived on an island and scientists had recently discovered a plague that would kill 97 percent of the island's residents. The scientists determined that 3 percent of the island's inhabitants are immune to the plague and will survive. Also, the scientists know how to create an antidote for the plague that will prevent people from being harmed, but the antidote needs to be made by using enzymes from the people who are immune, and they will die in the process of creating an antidote.

The students who received green coins are immune to the plague and those who received red coins will soon die if they do not receive an antidote. The professor told the class to determine what the group should do. This set off an intense debate.

The students with red coins felt that the decision should be based upon what is best for the group and the people who are immune should be killed to create an antidote. The students with green coins felt it would be unfair to have their lives sacrificed to save others. After around 20 minutes of heated debate, no agreement could be reached.

Then the professor collected all the coins and passed out sealed envelopes. He told the students to leave the envelopes sealed. Each envelope contained either a red coin or green coin, but we didn't know what color our coin was. We were told to play the game again and decide what to do. When nobody knew how the group's decision was going to affect them personally, it changed the tone and dynamics of the game. It only took about 2 minutes of discussion for the group to arrive at a unanimous decision. The group decided that the lives of the 3 percent of the immune people should be sacrificed to save the 97 percent of the people who will die if an antidote is not created.

John Rawls felt that to find justice, there needs to be rational self-interest plus impartiality. He also felt that justice involves choosing what provides the maximum benefit to those who have minimal advantages. The philosopher John Stuart Mill felt decisions should be based upon what creates the greatest good for the group.

Many of the problems affecting our world are like the Rawls Game. Decisions that create the greatest good or provide benefits to those who are disadvantaged are sometimes made difficult by the self-interests of a few. The wealth, power, and influence of a few often supersedes what is best for the majority. The disadvantaged may suffer when the advantaged use their privileges to increase their advantages at the expense of the disadvantaged.

The right decisions tend to become clearer when we focus on what creates the greatest good for the majority. If we had a veil of ignorance and did not know our circumstances, we would more likely make fairer decisions that are better for society.

The dynamics of group empathy is often affected by narcissism. Narcissism is empathy for oneself. Narcissism can be healthy, but excessive narcissism can be harmful. People who have excessive narcissism are called narcissists.

Narcissists

Narcissists are people who lack emotional empathy. People tend to believe narcissists have a big ego. A narcissist may reveal themselves by showing a big ego, but not always. Some narcissists are covert narcissists who are good at acting like they have empathy.

A covert narcissist may appear to be humble and kind – but only until you do something they don't like and then they may reveal their true toxic nature. Overt narcissists are easier to recognize because they like to brag (and often exaggerate) about how smart, connected, talented, attractive, or wealthy they are.

Some amount of narcissism is healthy, but excessive narcissism can be harmful. The most extreme narcissists are known as malignant narcissists. Unhealthy narcissism can be a personality disorder. *The Diagnostic and Statistical Manual of Mental Disorders* says a person has narcissistic personality disorder if they have 5 or more of these characteristics:

- Grandiose sense of their self-importance; exaggerates their achievements or talents.
- Preoccupied with fantasies of unlimited success, power, brilliance, beauty, or ideal love.
- Believes they are special and can only be understood by special or high-status people.
- Has an excessive need for admiration.
- Has a sense of entitlement. They expect to be treated better or treated special.
- Exploits and takes advantage of others.
- Lacks empathy; fails to identify the feelings and needs of others.
- Envious of others or believes people envy them.
- Shows arrogant, haughty behavior or attitudes.

Narcissists may wear different personality masks to hide their true nature. Narcissists are often described as being "wolves in sheep's clothing." By changing their persona, narcissists can be appealing to many different kinds of people. Narcissists may quickly develop friendships by customizing their persona to the person they are appealing to.

Narcissists can be good actors. When you meet a narcissist, you may feel like you have met a close friend or a soul mate. You may feel you have a deep rapport with them. However, the narcissist may just be reflecting you back to yourself, or they may be tailoring their personality to become the kind of person you are looking for.

A person who has a relationship with a narcissist may not realize how superficial the friendship is. Narcissists often use flattery to get people to like them. Narcissists are often described as being like chameleons because of how quickly they can change their persona.

Some narcissists seem to have a "Dr. Jekyll and Mr. Hyde personality." Their Dr. Jekyll side is often charming and engaging and is the personality that most people see. The Mr. Hyde side tends to mainly be seen by the people who are closest to the narcissist or people who the narcissist targets for abuse.

Narcissists can be very critical. They may claim to be perfectionists, but in reality, narcissists are imperfectionists. Nothing may ever be good enough to satisfy them. They constantly look for ways to criticize others. Their criticism is not meant to be constructive. Narcissists build themselves up by tearing others down.

Narcissists want to seem like they are the most talented person in the room. They may be jealous and may look for ways to discredit people who are better than them. They may criticize predecessors if the narcissist feels the predecessor receives more admiration. Narcissists tend to surround themselves with people who will agree with them.

Narcissists are very poor at self-reflecting. They tend to have an overinflated view of themselves. Narcissists like to take credit for things they have little or nothing to do with, and at the same time, narcissists will blame others for problems the narcissist caused.

People close to a narcissist may be treated like an extension of the narcissist instead of as individuals who have their own needs. In psychology, this is known as a narcissistic extension. A narcissist may expect their extensions to provide an endless supply of admiration and also be like a representative of the narcissist. Often the spouse and children of a narcissist become extensions and the narcissist may be very controlling and critical of them.

Family members may be expected to uphold the false façade of the narcissist. In public, the narcissist may seem to be an ideal parent or an ideal spouse, but their own family members may see them much differently. A narcissist may be loved by people who don't really know them, and hated by people who do really know them.

Narcissists may be self-absorbed and childish. They may act like the world revolves around them and others don't matter. They tend to be selfish and sometimes engage in bullying tactics. Narcissists tend to lack emotional maturity.

In dysfunctional families, some members may learn to compensate for deficiencies of other members of the family. For example, if a parent lacks empathy, then a child may need to develop greater levels of empathy to tolerate their parent's lack of empathy. Narcissists tend to raise children who become codependents or narcissists. Narcissists sometimes favor one child over another. The favored child might become a narcissist and the other child may become a codependent who tries hard to please.

Narcissists tend to find partners who are codependents. It's like a symbiotic relationship. Narcissists need empathetic partners who are willing to tolerate their lack of empathy, and codependents are used to being around narcissists who create one-sided relationships where the codependent shares empathy without receiving empathy in return.

An Impersonal Pan Pizza

A narcissist may know when their actions are causing pain to others, but inside the narcissist may feel indifferent about the harm they are causing. Sometimes people who lack empathy may feel pleasure by harming others. Narcissists and sociopaths both lack empathy. Narcissists tend to be less aware of how they affect people. A sociopath tends to be more strategic and cunning. A narcissist tends to be more impulsive.

Narcissists may use tactics to influence the empathy of others. For example, narcissists like to falsely portray themselves as a victim. They do this to appeal to the empathy of others so as to receive their help or sympathy. Narcissists are drawn to gullible, empathetic people who are easy to control and manipulate. Narcissists like to use people who don't have healthy boundaries. Narcissists look for people who are like low hanging fruit and are easy to take advantage of.

A narcissist may have a grooming process to find empathetic people. For example, they may share "secrets" about difficulties they experienced or situations where the narcissist claims to be a victim. A narcissist might invent situations that are similar to experiences the other person has had. The narcissist's personal stories might be lies or may be greatly distorted.

A potential victim might react with sympathy and feel closer to the narcissist who shared their "secret." The future victim may lower their guard and share their own personal secrets with the narcissist. That information might be used later by the narcissist to control and manipulate their victim.

When someone shares a lot of personal information about themselves soon after you meet them, then it may be a sign they are a narcissist. Or this could be a sign they are a codependent. Either way it may indicate a person who won't respect your boundaries (a narcissist) or a person who lacks boundaries (a codependent).

Narcissists tend to be on their best behavior in the early stages of a relationship. They may seem like a prince charming. Once the victim has bonded and feels invested in the relationship, then over time a narcissist starts to reveal their toxic nature.

Narcissists use many techniques to manipulate people. The techniques tend to fall into three main categories known as "FOG." – Fear, Obligation, and Guilt.

A narcissist may threaten a person or they may talk about bad times, and focus on negativity, or fears related to the future. A narcissist may cause someone to question their own sanity.

When a narcissist does something good it often comes with strings attached so that they can make people feel obligated to them and they will pull on those obligation strings to use others. Narcissists will often engage in destructive criticism that involves calling people names, putting people down, or engaging in shame and guilt trips directed towards others who they are trying to control or discredit.

Narcissists may use your core values to shame you. For example, you may be a person who is honest and generous and a narcissist may claim that you are selfish and dishonest. By attacking your core values, they cause you to defend yourself. Invariably, the narcissist keeps disagreeing with whatever you say as you go around in circles trying to prove yourself. When someone is playing the role of devil's advocate by saying things that are not true, you are probably dealing with a toxic personality, and the best course of action is to disengage from and avoid further contact with them.

Narcissists tend to be overly concerned by how they appear to others. For example, a narcissist may choose a trophy spouse who is attractive or successful so that the narcissist can use their partner as a way to impress others.

Narcissists may treat people like objects and take advantage of them. They can treat people like pawns in a chess game and keep them around as long as they serve a purpose. A narcissist can use and discard people and not feel any sense of guilt or regret.

Empathy helps create lasting relationships. Without empathy there are fewer bonds in a relationship. To a narcissist, relationships only have value as long as a person is useful.

A narcissist's level of bonding towards their spouse might be similar to how a person may love a sports car. They may like and enjoy the car and how they feel when they are with the car. They may take care of the car. But when the car starts to get old and rusty, the car can be easily replaced by a newer model and soon forgotten. Narcissists can quickly discard "friends" because they have no empathetic bonds with those "friends."

Narcissists sometimes make themselves look empathetic to bring praise to themselves. For example, a narcissist might donate money to a charity in exchange for recognition. It is unlikely a narcissist would donate money anonymously to help someone (or if they did, the narcissist would look for ways to make their "anonymous gift" become publicly known).

Narcissists may experience a physiological condition known as splitting. Splitting causes people to view things in black and white terms. A narcissist may see the world as being great or as being terrible. A minor misunderstanding with a narcissist can quickly cause them to view a friend as an enemy.

Empathetic people look for ways to cooperate and resolve issues. Narcissists like conflict and drama and get energy by draining other people of their energy. Narcissists are often described as being "emotional vampires." Narcissists may put people into no-win situations known as double binds. People can feel like they have to walk on eggshells to avoid upsetting a narcissist.

Narcissists like to come out ahead regardless of the cost to others. People with empathy are willing to compromise and reach a solution where both sides win. Narcissists like to milk a conflict for all it is worth and are less likely to structure deals that are fair to both sides.

Most human emotions fall on a spectrum. For example, consider the emotion of anger.

Most people become angry slowly over time. However, a narcissist tends to skip many of the stages of anger and will quickly become enraged. Sometimes even minor situations can cause a narcissist to be enraged.

Their sudden rage tends to occur when the narcissist feels they are being criticized or disrespected. This causes them to feel their ego has been injured and this is known as a narcissistic injury and the rage they experience is called narcissistic rage. If you ever witness this sudden change in the demeanor of a narcissist, it can be quite frightening. A narcissist can go from being happy to enraged very quickly.

Narcissists can control their rage at times. A narcissist might rage at someone in private but avoid showing rage when others are around. They may also hide their rage behind a false persona. Sometimes narcissists are passive aggressive. They may use the silent treatment to put someone in a form of solitary emotional confinement.

Narcissists seem to be coated in Teflon and can weasel out of problems they are responsible for. Nothing seems to stick to them. Narcissists are masters of deflection. When they do something wrong, they distort and exaggerate things in other directions and will redirect a conversation about problems related to them into issues about others. Narcissists want to be in charge of the podium so that they can control the narrative. It can be difficult to hold a narcissist accountable because narcissists are masterful at distorting reality.

Narcissists may misuse nuances of language. They use tactics that do not conform to the norms of empathetic people. For example, a narcissist may make statements in the form of a leading question. They might insult someone by using questions or telling lies in the form of a question. If they are confronted for making an abusive or misleading statement, they can deny responsibility and claim they were only asking a question.

A narcissist may get caught being abusive or dishonest and then claim they were "only joking" and may suggest the offended party "can't take a joke" or is "too sensitive." This shifts responsibility away from a narcissist's actions and redirects the misunderstanding onto the attacked person. Narcissists may use innuendos to subtly insult or disparage others. After criticizing someone, a narcissist might insincerely compliment them to avoid looking too critical.

Narcissists sometimes use partial truths to tell lies. They may say something that is 90% false but when confronted about lying, they point out what is true about what they said and then claim you misunderstood them. Often narcissists tell lies full of ambiguous things that let them clarify and change the meaning of the lie later.

Narcissists also lie by omission. They avoid telling you things you may want to know. They knowingly allow misunderstandings to occur. By not clarifying the truth, they mislead people but can claim they didn't lie because they may not have said anything that was untrue.

Narcissist are masters of insinuations and backhanded compliments. For example, a narcissist may call someone fat and ugly by saying "I would never say that you are fat and ugly." They may insult someone with a compliment such as "That dress looks really good on you; it would look even better if you lost some weight."

Narcissists use triangulation to create jealousy or conflicts between others. A narcissist triangulates by becoming a messenger between two people, or they may use one person to be their messenger to another person. Second-hand conversations are often used to spread false information or create misunderstandings.

Narcissists also use selective memory. When they are caught lying or doing something wrong they may claim to have no memory about what you are talking about, or they will distort or change the facts and claim to remember something different from what occurred.

People are not always certain about their memories and a narcissist takes advantage of this. For example, you might be 95 percent confident that your memory is correct and the narcissist may act like they are 150 percent certain that their memory is correct. The confidence that a narcissist has in their own incorrect memories (or lies) can cause others with accurate memories to doubt their own memories.

Narcissists tend to attack someone else's beliefs and opinions. Narcissist seem to feel their own beliefs and opinions are facts, and anyone who disagrees with them is wrong.

Narcissists are sometimes pathological liars. They lack empathy and it is easier for them to lie without feeling any guilt. Narcissists can look right into your eyes and lie and their lack of scruples makes it seem like they are telling you the truth.

A study at the University of Southern California appears to show that pathological liars have brains that make them good liars. In the study, researchers scanned brains of pathological liars and found they had 25.7% more prefrontal white matter. The study also showed that liars had 14.2 percent less prefrontal gray matter. The gray matter appears to affect morals and conscience. It takes more work for someone to pull off complex lies than to tell the truth, and this may be why pathological liars may develop brains with more white matter. The extra white matter may give them more processing power to be good liars. They may have a brain that makes it easier for them to lie and at the same time has less pullback from a conscience.

Narcissists also tend to have a distorted view of reality. At times they can be paranoid and delusional. They tend to project their distorted view of the world onto others. Sometimes narcissists try to distort and control the reality of others. To distort reality, narcissists may engage in pathetical lying, exaggeration or minimization techniques, and gaslighting.

Gaslighting is when a person tries to distort the reality of another person. Exaggeration techniques tend to use strong words such as "always" or "never" to distort the significance of something. Minimization techniques involve denying something and rationalizing something to downplay its significance. Pathological lying may be a compulsive habit where someone lies even when there may not be a reason to lie, or they exaggerate and stretch the truth.

Narcissists can be paranoid, delusional, dishonest, illogical people. Yet, a narcissist may not seem to be illogical or delusional because they hide their chaotic personalities behind a mask of sanity and appear to be level-headed while they engage in crazy-making activities. A person who spends much time around a narcissist can feel like they are going crazy.

The "dark triad" is a term in psychology used to describe dangerous individuals who lack empathy. The dark triad focuses on three personality traits: narcissism, Machiavellianism, and psychopathy. Narcissism is characterized by pride, egotism, grandiosity, and a lack of empathy. Machiavellianism is when a person focuses on their own self-interests and manipulates and exploits others by using deception and disregarding morality. Psychopathy is characterized by anti-social behavior, selfishness, impulsivity, callousness and remorselessness.

People are often taken by surprise by a narcissist because narcissists can hide their true nature. Sometimes it can be difficult to determine when someone is a narcissist, until enough time passes to see their true colors. Narcissists are great at telling people what they want to hear. Narcissists can be charismatic, create false masks, and appear to be charming, engaging, and likeable. Narcissists can even seem to have empathy by mimicking characteristics of empathy. However, they don't feel emotional empathy; they are only acting like they feel empathetic emotions.

A narcissist's lack of empathy may be revealed during stressful situations. A narcissist may overreact and show their lack of empathy when they feel angry or humiliated. They can have a strong temper, and be very disrespectful. In moments like this, the Mr. Hyde side of the narcissist may come out. When a person shows uncontrolled rage that quickly develops, they are showing their lack of empathy. When a person deflects and doesn't take responsibility for their own actions, this is often the sign of a narcissist.

History is full of examples of narcissists who gain power and then cause significant problems. The world's most despised man is probably Adolph Hitler. For a period of time, Hitler was very popular and well-liked in Germany. He was very charismatic and good at telling people what they wanted to hear. Outside of Germany, Hitler was feared and nations appeased him for a while hoping to avoid conflict. Hitler was likely a malignant narcissist.

Joseph McCarthy became one of America's most harmful senators who ruined people's reputations and careers with his false accusations. For a period of time, he had great control and power over others as he spread fear and polarized the nation. People were afraid to stand up to him because they feared they might become his next target.

Attitudes and Traits of Narcissists (9)
www.BluntHonest.com/Attitudes

Narcissistic Relationships (7, 8)
www.BluntHonest.com/Relate

Logical Fallacies

"We only go around in circles in Wonderland, but we always end up where we started."
– Mad Hatter, Alice in Wonderland

Logical fallacies are errors in reasoning. A person who uses logical fallacies may appear to be reasonable even though they are being illogical. Statements based on logical fallacies might not hold up once you apply logic to them. Logical fallacies are sometimes used by narcissists to win arguments or to influence others.

Donald Trump often uses logical fallacies. For example, Trump often criticizes people by using derogatory names. Attacking a person rather than evaluating and debating the merits of their ideas is a logical fallacy known as the "ad hominem" fallacy.

Trump claims lots of people agree with him. He brags about crowds of people and high approval ratings. He often uses the "bandwagon" logical fallacy. This fallacy implies that the popularity of something proves the validity of it. However, if a million people believe in a bad idea, it is still a bad idea. In the Netherlands in 1637, people were paying more for tulip bulbs than for houses because everyone thought the price of tulips would keep going up. When the tulip market crashed it became obvious that the popularity of an idea does not make it true.

A "false dilemma" fallacy assumes that only two choices are available even though there are other options. George W. Bush used this fallacy to convince America to start a war with Iraq. He falsely claimed that Iraq had weapons of mass destruction. Then he convinced people we only had two choices: attack Iraq or wait to be attacked by Iraq. He made it sound like war was inevitable. Even if Iraq had weapons of mass destruction, it didn't mean they would use them. There are diplomatic options available and war is not always required.

When Bush was trying to get other countries to participate in the Iraq War, he told them *"You are either with us, or you are with the terrorists."* Let's consider how illogical that statement is: If a country chooses to remain neutral, it does not mean they support terrorism.

The Bush administration ignored information that did not fit their views and may have intentionally mislead the nation about weapons that did not exist. The documentary film *War of Lies* shows that lies may have been fabricated to justify the Iraq War. The movie *Fair Game* shows how valid intelligence information was ignored and suppressed in order to justify the war. The Iraq War cost $3 trillion and 500,000 people died. As you can see, logical fallacies can be dangerous, expensive, and harmful.

The "argument of ignorance" fallacy is often used by climate deniers. This fallacy says that without certainty, something cannot be accepted. However, it is common in science (and in life) to base decisions on high probability without certainty. Yet climate deniers will focus on low levels of uncertainty rather than high probabilities. Climate deniers often use logical fallacies to create false conclusions or cause doubts.

A "straw man" fallacy involves misstating a person's position in order to defeat the misstated position, rather than debate the person's actual position. "Alternative facts" fallacy is when people create false or distorted facts to justify their beliefs. A "magnification" fallacy is when someone exaggerates things. Someone may claim something is the biggest, best, or worst even though their claims are not based on facts.

Sometimes a person makes a statement that is not based on evidence and then tries to use their unproven statement as proof. This is known as a "circular logic" fallacy.

A "guilt by association" fallacy tries to discredit a person by saying they have the same character traits or are responsible or tied to the actions of another person. This fallacy tries to imply guilt without sufficient evidence of the guilt being justified.

A "correlation proves causation" fallacy is when someone claims that when two events occur together they must have a cause and effect relationship, However, correlation does not prove causation.

Logical fallacies can cause conversations to go around in circles and nothing gets resolved. When a person uses logical fallacies and others attempt to bring logic into the conversation, sometimes the illogical person may attempt to avoid logic by switching from one logical fallacy to another, or they will keep reusing the same invalid logic.

Around 150 different kinds of logical fallacies exist. Logical fallacies tend to be based on unproven assumptions, may use biases and prejudices, and often appeal to a person's emotions instead of a person's reasoning. Logical fallacies can mislead people. Once you are aware of common fallacies it is easier to recognize them.

The Iraq War video montage shows how logical fallacies were used to justify the war and the consequences of the war. The other montage gives examples of logical fallacies and shows how Trump uses logical fallacies.

Iraq War (9)
www.BluntHonest.com/Iraq

Logical Fallacies (8, 9)
www.BluntHonest.com/Logical

You Americans All Look Alike

I used to work with a guy named Jim, who was Japanese. One day, Jim said to me *"You Americans all look alike."*

I couldn't believe what Jim had said. I think Americans have the most diverse range of physical appearances among any population in the world. We have a variety of hair colors, skin tones, eye colors, body shapes and facial features. When I look at Asians, I see mostly black hair, similar faces, similar eyes, and similar skin tones.

I said to Jim, *"How can you say that? Asian people look more alike than Americans do."* Then Jim said *"Asian people all look different, but you Americans all look alike."*

Surely Jim didn't know what he was talking about. I decided to do some research.

As I met people who grew up in other countries I asked them if they thought Americans looked alike and I was surprised by their response. People from Africa, Asia, and the Middle East were telling me they thought Americans all looked alike, but they felt that people who were from their parts of the world looked different from each other. However, when I looked at people from Asia, Africa, and the Middle East they seemed to look alike to me.

This puzzled me, and then I remembered when I was a child, I could go into a classroom and see the differences among the other kids my age. But in a room full of adults I had trouble telling adults apart because often adults seemed to look alike to me. Sometimes adults would come into a room of kids and say, *"I have trouble telling you kids apart, you kids all look alike."*

Then I thought about animals of other species. When I look at a flock of birds, all the birds look alike to me. But those birds can recognize their mates and find them among the thousands of birds.

Eventually I came up with a theory to explain what was happening:

> *We notice the differences in people who are similar to us and we notice the similarities in people who are different from us.*

Later, I found out that my theory is related to a concept in psychology known as "outgroup homogeneity effect" where we tend to view others who are part of another group as being similar and we view people who are part of our group as being more diverse.

Daniel Levin, PhD, a cognitive psychologist, has done facial recognition experiments and found that people often have difficulty recognizing a face of someone who is in a different racial group and this is known as "cross-race recognition deficit."

This deficit can cause problems in courtrooms. Eyewitness testimony can be filled with errors, especially when a witness is asked to identify a person who is from a different racial group. Sometimes witnesses accuse innocent people of a crime. People are sometimes convicted and punished because of recognition errors of an eyewitness.

Sometimes we assume that people who appear to look the same are the same. This can contribute to prejudices and stereotypes we form of others.

When you perceive that someone is similar to you, perhaps it is easier to feel empathy towards them. Perhaps you are more willing to appreciate and respect the differences of people who are similar to you. Perhaps when people are different from you it is more difficult to feel empathy towards them or to notice and appreciate their differences.

It's easier to put yourself in the shoes of someone who is similar to you than in the shoes of someone who is much different than you.

Justice is supposed to be blind. People are supposed to be treated fairly and equally. If two people committed the same crime then they should be given the same punishment. However, judges and juries are human. Humans experience different degrees of empathy based on differences and similarities they have with the person who is accused.

Sometimes whether a person is convicted and punished or set free may hinge upon things that have nothing to do with the facts of the case. A person's race, age, sex, clothing, tattoos, level of attractiveness, socio-economic status, level of education, or perceived level of intelligence, may affect the impressions and decisions of the judge or jury.

Studies have shown that judges who have daughters appear to be more lenient on women who are being tried in their courts. Our level of empathy and prejudices have an impact on the outcome of trials.

Sometimes cultural biases may affect outcomes of trials. For example, if a woman was abused for years by her husband and she shot and killed him, a jury may feel she acted in self-defense or was temporarily insane because of the abuse, and the jury may find her not guilty and doesn't punish her.

But if the same circumstances occurred where a man was being abused by a woman for years and he shot and killed her, and all the evidence was identical and the same jury heard the same evidence, the outcome of the trial might be different.

People on the jury might say a man should have left that abusive relationship. A man should never hurt a woman. That same jury who may let a woman go free for killing a man under similar circumstances, might feel that the man's actions are unacceptable and the man should be punished.

The scales of justice are sometimes tipped according to the level of empathy a judge or a jury has for a person. Empathy is not blind and therefore justice is not truly blind

These illegal aliens all look alike!

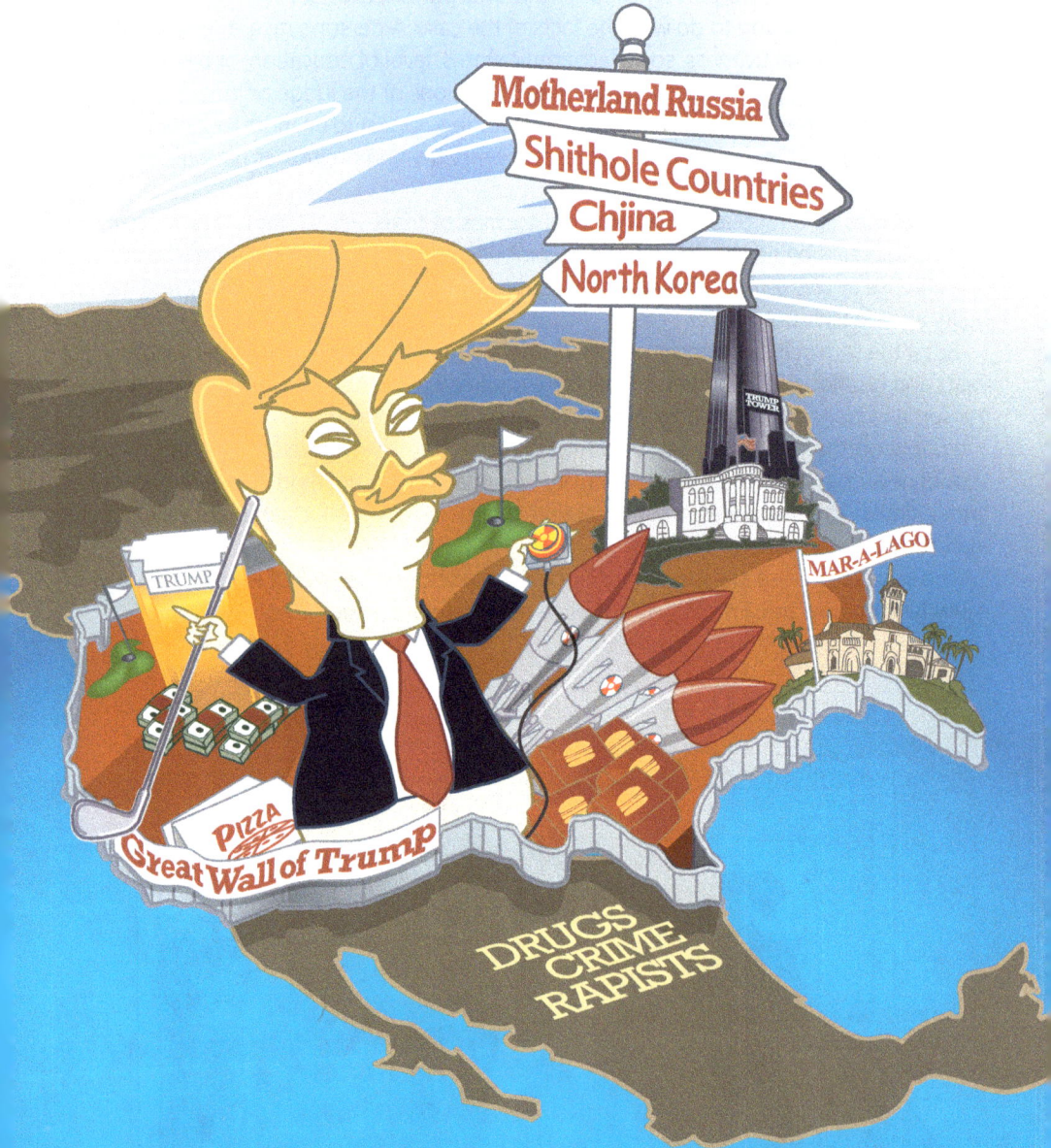

Trump's View of the World

The Scorpion and the Frog Fable

A scorpion asked a frog to let him hop on her back and take him across a river. The frog said *"How do I know you won't sting me?"* The scorpion said *"I won't. Also, I don't know how to swim and if I stung you I would drown."* The frog let the scorpion onto her back. While she was swimming, the scorpion stung her. As she was dying she screamed *"Why did you do that?"* The scorpion replied *"I'm a scorpion, that's what I do."*

A person's past actions often indicate how they will be in the future. False promises are easy to make. Putting our trust in someone who lacks empathy can put us at risk.

Donald Trump seems racist at times. In 1973 and 1978 the Trump Organization was accused of violating the Fair Housing Act by avoiding renting apartments to minorities. In 1983, *The New York Times* reported that Trump properties were disproportionately filled with white tenants (95% of their tenants were white). John O'Donnell worked with Trump and wrote a book about Trump. His book said Trump felt "Laziness is a trait in blacks."

In 1989, 5 boys (ages of 14 to 16) were charged with raping a white woman in Central Park. The boys (four were black and one was Hispanic) became known as the "Central Park 5." Trump called them *"crazed misfits"* and he paid for full page newspaper ads urging that the death penalty punishment be brought back. Trump said *"I want to hate these murderers and I always will... Maybe hate is what we need if we're gonna get something done."* Lawyers for the five defendants said that Trump's advertisements had inflamed public opinion.

The boys were convicted and spent between 6 to 13 years in jail. In 2002, another man confessed to the crime and DNA evidence confirmed his guilt. Michael W. Warren, an attorney for one of the falsely accused boys, said Trump *"owes a real apology to this community and to the young men and their families."* In 2002 demonstrators gathered outside of Trump Tower to protest his actions towards the innocent men. Trump remained unapologetic and said *"I don't mind if they picket. I like pickets."* In 2013, a documentary film showed how the Central Park 5 were unfairly treated. Trump said the film was *"one sided"* and didn't explain their *"horrific crimes."* In 2014, the city of New York paid a settlement to the Central Park 5. Trump criticized the settlement and said the men are not *"angels"* and the payment was like a *"heist."*

When Trump was running for president, he told blacks they should vote for him saying *"What the hell do you have to lose?"* After polls showed that only 2% of African American voters supported Trump, he changed his tone and said he wanted *"the vote of every African American citizen struggling in our country today who wants a different future."*

In Florida, Trump told Haitian voters *"Whether you vote for me or not I really want to be your biggest champion."* In a debate he was asked why he dropped his 5-year quest to discredit Barack Obama's birthplace and Trump said *"When you talk about healing, I think that I've developed very, very good relationships over the last little while with the African-American community."* During his campaign, Trump posed with the rainbow Pride flag and promised to *"...do everything in my power to protect our LGBTQ citizens from hateful and foreign ideology."*

After he was President, Trump said some of the white supremacists in Charlottesville were *"very fine people."* He said a black football player who knelt during national anthems to call attention to the Black Lives Matter movement was a *"son of a bitch"* who should be fired. Lawmakers said Trump called African nations *"shithole countries"* and called Haiti a *"shithole country."* He reinstated a ban on transgender people in the military, appointed judges and high-ranking officials who have a history of opposing LGBTQ equality, and fired all members of the Presidential Advisory Council on HIV/AIDS.

Pride and Prejudice

Donald Trump has made news for controversies related to race, ethnic groups, women, religion, orientation, and people with disabilities. Some people feel that Trump is authentic. Often, authenticity is in the eye of the beholder. When Trump says things that seem prejudiced, someone who shares similar beliefs may feel he is being authentic. Some people think Trump expresses pride and patriotism and others think he is prejudiced. Now, let's consider the difference between pride and prejudice.

Pride creates self-confidence and is motivational. Healthy pride is humble, respectful, and grateful. People may find pride in their religion, gender, race, children, accomplishments, and sexual orientation. People may feel pride for their city, culture, and heritage. National anthems often express pride for one's country.

However, sometimes people are arrogant. When someone thinks they are superior or entitled, their excessive pride may become prejudice. It's important to remember that every person is a member of the human race. All of us are Earthlings. Every man, woman, child, and creature are children of the planet Earth.

Mostly Healthy Pride (6,7)
www.BluntHonest.com/Pride

Racism & Tolerance (8)
www.BluntHonest.com/Racism

Religious Strife & Harmony (8)
www.BluntHonest.com/Strife

Ethnic Prejudice & Tolerance (8)
www.BluntHonest.com/Ethnic

Gay Prejudice & Tolerance (8)
www.BluntHonest.com/Gay

Ableism & Acceptance (8)
www.BluntHonest.com/Able

Speciesism & Kindness (8)
www.BluntHonest.com/Animal

Objectification and Gender Issues

Sometimes, people or animals are treated like objects instead of being treated like living beings who have feelings. When a person or animal is objectified, their value is associated with how they can serve a purpose and be used by others.

The word "objectification" is most often used to describe how women are treated. However, objectification can harm both women and men.

In Western society women tend to be objectified as sex objects and men tend to be objectified as success objects. Objectification harms more people than just the group that is being objectified. The objectification of women harms women, but it also harms children and men. The objectification of men harms men, but it also harms children and women.

For example, objectification of women's looks affects the self-confidence of women and girls. Physical objectification can also make it more difficult for men and women to develop meaningful relationships.

Often objectification is subtle and may occur as an undertone of society. Objectification harms those who are objectified and can also harm the people who are doing the objectification. For example, people who view others as sex objects may become sex addicts.

Gender issues are further complicated by how people talk and deal with them. There seems to be a desire to only focus on the plight of one gender without considering concerns of the other gender. Sometimes the concerns of one gender results in the blaming and vilification of the other gender. In reality, women's issues are affected by men's issues and men's issues are affected by women's issues. Yet often we fail to see how gender roles and biases intertwine and affect each other.

Women Stereotypes (7)
www.BluntHonest.com/Women

Success Objects, Abuse of Men (8)
www.BluntHonest.com/Success

Men Stereotypes (7)
www.BluntHonest.com/Men

Sex Objects (8)
www.BluntHonest.com/Sex

We Are All Time Travelers

"One of the great revelations of the Space Age has been the perspective it has given humanity on ourselves. When we see the Earth from space, we see ourselves as a whole. We see the unity and not the divisions. It is such a simple image with a compelling message. One planet. One human race. We are here together and we need to live together with tolerance and respect. We must become global citizens. Our only boundaries are the way we see ourselves. The only borders, the way we see each other...We are all time travelers, journeying together into the future. But let us work together to make that future a place we want to visit." – Stephen Hawking

Dehumanization

Dehumanization is similar to objectification but may be worse. Dehumanization lowers the status of another living being to a point where we don't feel empathy for them and we may feel justified in harming them. Dehumanization helps people suspend their empathy towards others.

When people reduce their empathy, they may become like narcissists towards the dehumanized person or group. Sometimes people are situational narcissists. They may have empathy for some people or animals and lack empathy for others. This is different from narcissists who have a general lack of emotional empathy. Narcissists can encourage empathetic people to become situational narcissists. Often a dehumanization process occurs to turn empathetic people into situational narcissists.

It is harder for people to mistreat others or to accept mistreatment of others who they have empathy for. The dehumanization process tends to be gradual and happens over time. Often, dehumanization begins small such as calling people names or making derogatory jokes about those who are being targeted. Tactics that involve "killing the messenger" or "guilt by association" are sometimes used to dehumanize someone or to suppress evidence of dehumanization. Dehumanization is disrespect.

Over time, dehumanization tactics may evolve into taking away rights from those who are dehumanized. Then it may advance into higher degrees of dehumanization such as imprisonment, torture, or killing of those who are dehumanized. Prejudice is sometimes caused by dehumanization. Prejudice is a way to control or suppress empathy.

Sometimes, dehumanization may cause people to become abusive towards the dehumanized group. Sometimes dehumanization causes people to have apathy or indifference towards the targeted group. Dehumanization helped people to justify owning slaves. Dehumanization lets people use and slaughter animals without feeling guilt. Dehumanization helps people justify wars and allows people to accept and participate in genocides.

The Nazis dehumanized the Jews. The book "Eichmann in Jerusalem: A Report on the Banality of Evil" (Penguin Classics, 2006) describes how the cruelty of the Nazis was possible. When people lack empathy, their apathy and indifference make it possible for an ordinary person to participate in cruel actions or to allow cruelty to occur. A person may not have evil or malicious intent, but rather an indifference to the harm that is occurring.

One thing that often occurs before war and during wars is a process of dehumanizing the other side. Propaganda and news coverage is used to reduce people's empathy towards the other side. Making others seem less than human makes it easier to harm or kill them without feeling remorse. When leaders and public media dehumanize the other side, this is often the beginning stages of a future conflict. It is common for both sides of a dispute to go through a dehumanization process.

The dehumanization process tries to invalidate the essence of who a person is. We tell ourselves if a person is bad then everything about the person is bad. If we feel the leader of a country is bad then we may think everyone in their country is bad. It's rare that anyone is 100 percent good or 100 percent bad. The dehumanization process is a form of splitting that can cause us to see things as being black or white, good or evil.

History is written by the victors of a conflict. Often the victors glorify themselves and demonize their enemies. Even though atrocities tend to occur on both sides of a conflict, the victors sweep their own atrocities under the rug while they focus on the atrocities of the side that lost.

The dehumanization process is often protected by the people who have power and who are responsible for the dehumanization. They know that anything that humanizes the other side is a threat to their agenda. For example, when videos leak about a government's abusive war tactics, you'll often hear the government claim the leak of the videos is a matter of national security, and the person who leaked evidence of the government's abuse is a traitor who is helping the enemy.

People who try to humanize the other side often get dehumanized in an attempt to discredit their opinions and actions. For example, in the United States, several states have passed laws to make it illegal to film or share videos of animals being harmed or abused on farms. Instead of taking steps to be humane and recognize the harm we are causing to animals, farm industries have gotten laws passed to hide the abuse from the public. People who expose the abuse of animals may be treated like criminals and prosecuted.

Whenever we dehumanize or objectify others, we become like narcissists. We look at the other side with black and white thinking. We turn others into objects and don't consider their feelings. We think we are smarter and better than others. We believe we can read their minds and interpret the motives of those we dehumanize. We think we are better than those we harm. We have no empathy for the other. We become callous and indifferent. We become like narcissists.

We can be extremely cruel and then deflect and ignore our own cruelty by focusing on the flaws of the other or by diminishing the individuality or worth of the other. We may also distort our reality to allow us to accept ourselves. We use cognitive dissonance to overlook our own flaws or our role in a conflict. We don't take responsibility or self-reflect because it is easier to dehumanize the other and focus on their flaws.

Dehumanization (9)
www.BluntHonest.com/Dehuman

Propaganda

George Orwell's book *1984*, shows how propaganda can be used to control people and distort their reality. His book showed a world where the government controlled language in order to control the thoughts of its citizens.

Often, propaganda occurs as part of dehumanization. Propaganda may involve calling people names, using derogatory jokes, or spreading rumors about the person or group being targeted. Sometimes propaganda involves forming organizations, hiring spokespeople, or creating music, films, books, or other methods of influencing the beliefs of others.

Before a war occurs, both sides of a conflict often engage in propaganda to dehumanize each other. Propaganda may justify a war and encourage people to support it. Propaganda is often full of misinformation. The other side may be shown as ruthless or immoral, or as being dumb or cowardly. The other side may be shown as having unfit parents who raise defective children. The culture or religion of a group may be misrepresented. When propaganda causes fear, people may make decisions based on emotions instead of reasoning.

During World War II, the Nazis created films dehumanizing the Jews. Japanese films showed Americans as a Mickey Mouse character who dropped bombs and tortured Japanese people. American films showed the Japanese as ruthless idiots.

Society may use propaganda to dehumanize groups of people, promote prejudice, and excuse the unfair treatment of the targeted groups. In the United States, the film *Birth of a Nation* had white actors who put on makeup to look black. That film portrayed the Klu Klux Klan as being heroic and it dehumanized black people.

Propaganda can influence elections by making a candidate's ideology more important than their ability to do a good job. Much of Trump's campaign focused on dehumanizing immigrants, Muslims, and Mexicans. His campaign appealed to people's fears and he told people that he was the only one who could solve our problems. He called his opponents names to dehumanize and dismiss them instead of thoughtfully discussing the issues.

In Trump's election campaign, social media data was used to target specific voters in key states and show them propaganda. This encouraged people to vote for Trump and discouraged them from voting for Clinton. Russia also used social media and fake news to sway the election towards Trump. In the 2016 election, 2,864,974 more people voted for Clinton than Trump, but Trump won because he got more electoral college votes.

In 2010, a Supreme Court ruling for Citizens United removed some limitations on political propaganda spending. This has increased "dark money" where people anonymously donate money to organizations to influence politics. Those organizations sometimes produce false or distorted propaganda and release it anonymously to avoid being held accountable. Election results can be swayed by these groups and some politicians give priority to serving the needs of special interest groups over the needs of the people they are supposed to represent.

Politics, *1984*, Social Media (9)
www.BluntHonest.com/Political

Societal & War Propaganda (8)
www.BluntHonest.com/Societal

Berate America Again

"America's darkest moments have come when economic arguments trumped moral principles." – Mike Pence, September 17, 2010.

Donald Trump said he will "Make America Great Again." That's a nice slogan, but talk is cheap and actions are more important than words. Based on Trump's actions, a more appropriate slogan would be "Berate America Again" or perhaps "Make America Hate Again."

Trump is excessively critical about our country, the people, and the institutions. He spends a lot of time invoking fear, anger, and resentment. He divides people. Trump often creates unnecessary conflicts and drama. These distractions make it more difficult for the country to achieve meaningful accomplishments.

Constructive criticism can be helpful at times. Constructive criticism is meant to build people up and help them be the best they can be. Constructive criticism is kind and honest and has a spirit of "let's work together to resolve important issues." However, the type of criticism Trump uses is often destructive. He embarrasses and humiliates people. He uses shame, threats and name-calling to intimidate, control, and use people. He exaggerates and distorts things to create "alternative facts" to justify his criticism.

Like many narcissists, Trump is profusive at dishing out heaps of criticism, but he is not able to tolerate criticism directed at him. Even constructive criticism towards him is not tolerated. When he is criticized, Trump launches excessive counter-attacks of criticism directed at the person who criticized him. In a tweet Trump said *"When someone attacks me, I always attack back...except 100x more. This has nothing to do with a tirade but rather a way of life!"*

Trump seems to view criticism like he views revenge. He said *"When you are in business you need to get even with people who screw you. You need to screw them back 15 times harder... go for the jugular, attack them in spades!"*

Perhaps there is another reason why Trump frequently uses the phrase "Make America Great Again." Those words were originally said by Ronald Reagan. However, Trump owns the rights to that phrase because he filed for a trademark on it in 2012. Anyone who wants to use that phrase for commercial purposes needs to get his permission and may need to pay him.

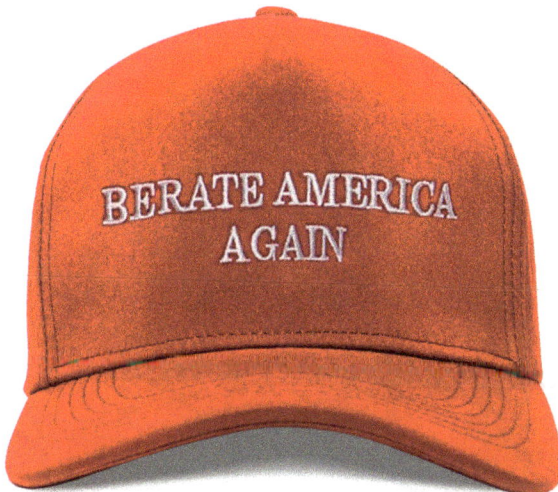

Head in the Sand

Most people tend to avoid conflict. If a problem doesn't directly affect them, they don't feel a need to speak up. They want to remain neutral and uninvolved. However, when people ignore problems, they indirectly allow problems to continue.

Elie Wiesel, winner of the Nobel peace prize, talked about neutrality in the face of a tormenter and said *"We must always take sides. Neutrality helps the oppressor, never the victim. Silence encourages the tormentor, never the tormented."*

Martin Niemöller spent 7 years in Nazi concentration camps. After the war ended, he gave a speech and said *"First they came for the Socialists, and I did not speak out— Because I was not a Socialist. Then they came for the Trade Unionists, and I did not speak out— Because I was not a Trade Unionist. Then they came for the Jews, and I did not speak out— Because I was not a Jew. Then they came for me—and there was no one left to speak for me."*

In 1951, while the United States was in the midst of McCarthyism, Maurice Ogden released a poem called "The Hangman" that talked about the perils of observing harm and doing nothing about it.

When Hannah Arendt wrote about the 1961 trial of Adolf Eichmann, a Nazi who helped organize the Holocaust, she used the phrase "the banality of evil" to describe how ordinary people may tolerate or participate in evil actions by conforming to mass opinions, obeying orders, or by being thoughtless.

Banality of Evil / Hangman Poem (9)
www.BluntHonest.com/Hang

Trump's Fondness for Vladimir Putin

The FBI determined the Russians meddled in the 2016 U.S. Presidential election. Trump has repeatedly denied any involvement in the scandal and has also claimed that no Russian interference occurred. Trump seems to compliment the Russians and have a soft spot for Russian President Vladimir Putin.

Rarely does Trump say anything negative about Putin. On a few occasions, Trump has made constructive or cautionary statements about Putin, but overall Trump seems to praise or defend Putin. Trump criticizes a lot of people and calls people names. However, when it comes to Putin, Trump is very complimentary.

Some of the words Trump has used to describe Putin include: *"Brilliant," "could not have been nicer," "done an amazing job," "so smart," "have to give him a lot of credit," "Putin treated me unbelievably well," "I get along with him fine," "Putin is a nicer person than I am," "In Terms of leadership, he is getting an 'A,'" "We get along great," "He's running his country and at least he's a leader, unlike what we have in this country," "I've always had a good feeling about him," "he called me a genius," "very nice," "Putin said good things about me," "he was a strong leader."*

In October of 2007, on *The Larry King Show*, Trump said *"Look at Putin – what he's doing with Russia – I mean, you know, what's going on over there. I mean this guy has done – whether you like him or don't like him – he's doing a great job in rebuilding the image of Russia and also rebuilding Russia, period."*

In Trump's 2011 book *Time to Get Tough*, Trump said *"Putin has big plans for Russia. He wants to edge out its neighbors so that Russia can dominate oil supplies to all of Europe. I respect Putin and Russians but cannot believe our leader (Obama) allows them to get away with so much...Hats off to the Russians."*

In June of 2013 Trump invited Putin to the Miss Universe pageant, and Trump tweeted *"Do you think Putin will be going to The Miss Universe Pageant in November in Moscow - if so, will he become my new best friend?"*

In November of 2013, on *MSNBC*, Trump talked about his relationship with Putin, *"I do have a relationship and I can tell you that he's very interested in what we're doing here today... He's probably very interested in what you and I are saying today, and I'm sure he's going to be seeing it in some form, but I do have a relationship with him and I think it's very interesting to see what's happened."*

On February 10, 2014, on *Fox & Friends*, Trump says Putin had contacted him, *"When I went to Russia with the Miss Universe pageant, (Putin) contacted me and was so nice. I mean, the Russian people were so fantastic to us...I'll just say this, they are doing – they're outsmarting us at many turns, as we all understand. I mean, their leaders are, whether you call them smarter or more cunning or whatever, but they're outsmarting us. If you look at Syria or other places, they're outsmarting us."*

On April 12, 2014, Trump told *Fox Business'* Eric Bolling that Putin treated him well while Trump was in Russia for *Miss Universe*. Trump said *"He could not have been nicer. He was so nice and so everything. But you have to give him credit that what he's doing for that country in terms of their world prestige is very strong."*

On December 20, 2015, on *ABC's This Week*, Trump was asked about allegations that Putin had ordered the killing of journalists and dissidents. Trump said *"But, in all fairness to Putin, you're saying he killed people. I haven't' seen that. I don't know that he has. Have you* been able to prove that? Do you know the names of the reporters that he's killed? Because I've been — you know, you've been hearing this, but I haven't seen the names. Now, I think it would be despicable if that took place, but I haven't' seen any evidence that he killed anybody in terms of reporters."

On January 26, 2016, *Fox Business'* Maria Bartiromo asked Trump about the findings of a British inquiry that said Putin "probably approved" the murder of Alexander Litvinenko. Trump said *"Have they found him guilty? I don't think they've found him guilty. If he did it, fine. But I don't know that he did it. You know, people are saying they think it was him, it might have been him, it could have been him. But Maria, in all fairness to Putin—I don't know. You know, and I'm not saying this because he says, 'Trump is brilliant and leading everybody' —the fact is that, you know, he hasn't been convicted of anything."*

At a rally in Ohio on October 27, 2016, Trump said it was not smart for Clinton to speak *"very badly of Putin."* When Bill O'Reilly called Putin a killer in February, 2017, Trump said *"There are a lot of killers...Do you think our country is so innocent? Do you think our country is so innocent?"*

Trump has praised leaders who are dictators, have a history of civil rights violations, or are very controlling of their people. Some of the leaders Trump has complimented include: Rodrigo Duterte, Xi Jinping, Abdel-Fattah el-Sissi, Recep Tayyip Erdogan, Kim Jong-un, and Vladimir Putin. People tend to identify with others who are like themselves. Perhaps Trump's affinity towards these kinds of leaders reveals some things about him.

In August 2016, Michael Morell, former acting director of the CIA, wrote in a *New York Times* op-ed, *"President Vladimir V. Putin of Russia was a career intelligence officer, trained to identify vulnerabilities in an individual and to exploit them... Mr. Putin played upon Mr. Trump's vulnerabilities by complimenting him... Mr. Putin is a great leader, Mr. Trump says, ignoring that he has killed and jailed journalists and political opponents, has invaded two of his neighbors and is driving his economy to ruin. Mr. Trump has also taken policy positions consistent with Russian, not American interests...In the intelligence business, we would say that Mr. Putin had recruited Mr. Trump as an unwitting agent of the Russian Federation."*

The Elephant in the Room

Covert narcissists are difficult to recognize because they may be good actors who can fake emotions. They may appear to be humble and empathetic.

Overt narcissists are easier to spot. They tend to have pompous, over-inflated egos and their lack of empathy is more apparent. When it comes to overt narcissists, you don't need a telescope to recognize them. Overt narcissists are easy to see. When someone looks like a narcissist, talks like a narcissist, and acts like a narcissist, they are a narcissist.

Even though a narcissist may not be directly targeting you with their abusive tactics, that doesn't mean you are safe. When a narcissist achieves a level of power and influence in your life, they can potentially be very dangerous to you.

Throughout history, the most significant and devastating events caused by mankind are often related to a lack of empathy on the part of the people who caused the problems. Great leaders have empathy. With great power comes great responsibility. Leaders who lack empathy are time bombs waiting to explode. Narcissists are often the elephant in the room. They are big, massive problems that nobody wants to recognize or deal with.

Trump Versus North Korea

A lot of conflict and drama has occurred with Trump's administration. Let's look at just one of the conflicts. Trump's conflict with Kim Jong-un, the leader of North Korea, shows what can happen when two narcissistic leaders go head to head.

Trump's words directed at North Korea reveals a lot of things about Trump. He seems to have an antagonistic attitude. It's almost as though Trump enjoys putting down and making fun of Kim Jong-un. He is threatening and egging on the leader of North Korea to create a conflict rather than looking for diplomatic solutions.

Here are things Trump has said about North Korea over the course of a year:

"North Korea just stated that it is in the final stages of developing a nuclear weapon capable of reaching parts of the U.S. It won't happen!"- Jan 2, 2017

"North Korea is looking for trouble. If China decides to help, that would be great. If not, we will solve the problem without them! U.S.A." – April 11, 2017

"There is a chance that we could end up having a major, major conflict with North Korea. Absolutely" – April 28, 2017

"North Korea best not make any more threats to the United States. They will be met with fire and fury like the world has never seen ... he has been very threatening beyond a normal state. They will be met with fire, fury and frankly power the likes of which this world has never seen before." – Aug 9, 2017

Military solutions are now fully in place, locked and loaded, should North Korea act unwisely. Hopefully Kim Jong-un will find another path!" – Aug 11, 2017

"The U.S. has been talking to North Korea, and paying them extortion money, for 25 years. Talking is not the answer," – Aug 30, 2017

"I spoke with President Moon of South Korea last night. Asked him how Rocket Man is doing. Long gas lines forming in North Korea. Too bad!" – Sep 17, 2017

On Sept 19, 2017, Trump gave his first speech at the United Nations and said this about North Korea:

"The scourge of our planet today is a small group of rogue regimes that violate every principle on which the United Nations is based. They respect neither their own citizens nor the sovereign rights of their countries.

"If the righteous many do not confront the wicked few, then evil will triumph. When decent people and nations become bystanders to history, the forces of destruction only gather power and strength.

"No one has shown more contempt for other nations and for the wellbeing of their own people than the depraved regime in North Korea. It is responsible for the starvation deaths of millions of North Koreans, and for the imprisonment, torture, killing, and oppression of countless more.

"We were all witness to the regime's deadly abuse when an innocent American college student, Otto Warmbier, was returned to America only to die a few days later. We saw it in the assassination of the dictator's brother using banned nerve agents in an international airport. We know it kidnapped a sweet 13-year-old Japanese girl from a beach in her own

country to enslave her as a language tutor for North Korea's spies.

"If this is not twisted enough, now North Korea's reckless pursuit of nuclear weapons and ballistic missiles threatens the entire world with unthinkable loss of human life.

"It is an outrage that some nations would not only trade with such a regime, but would arm, supply, and financially support a country that imperils the world with nuclear conflict. No nation on Earth has an interest in seeing this band of criminals arm itself with nuclear weapons and missiles.

"The United States has great strength and patience, but if it is forced to defend itself or its allies, we will have no choice but to totally destroy North Korea. Rocket Man is on a suicide mission for himself and for his regime. The United States is ready, willing and able, but hopefully this will not be necessary. That's what the United Nations is all about; that's what the United Nations is for. Let's see how they do.

"It is time for North Korea to realize that the denuclearization is its only acceptable future. The United Nations Security Council recently held two unanimous 15-0 votes adopting hard-hitting resolutions against North Korea, and I want to thank China and Russia for joining the vote to impose sanctions, along with all of the other members of the Security Council. Thank you to all involved.

"But we must do much more. It is time for all nations to work together to isolate the Kim regime until it ceases its hostile behavior."

On Sept 19, 2017, Hillary Clinton (Former Secretary of State) spoke on the *Late Show* with Stephen Colbert about what Trump had said in his UN speech. Clinton said:

"I thought it was very dark, dangerous. Not the kind of message that the leader of the greatest nation in the world should be delivering. You are both required to stand up for the values of what we believe in, democracy and opportunity, as a way to demonstrate clearly the United States remains the beacon that we want it to be.

"While of course when you face dangerous situations like what is happening in North Korea, to make it clear, your first approach should always be diplomatic.

"What I'd hoped the President would have said was something along the lines of, 'We view this as dangerous to our allies, to the region, and even to our countries. We call on all nations to work with us to try to end the threat posed by Kim Jong-un' and not call him Rocket Man, the old Elton John song, but to say clearly, we will not tolerate any attacks on our friends or ourselves. But you should lead with diplomacy. You should lead with the commitment to try to avoid conflict however you can."

Trump reacted to Clinton's constructive feedback by criticizing Clinton in an attempt to deflect attention away from himself and put the blame back on to Clinton. Trump tweeted:

"After allowing North Korea to research and build Nukes while Secretary of State (Bill C also), Crooked Hillary now criticizes." – 3:40 AM Sep 20, 2017.

Like many of the things Trump says, his tweet distorts things, omits relevant facts, and uses a logical fallacy. He also uses a derogatory moniker to dehumanize the person he is criticizing.

Trump's tweet makes it sound like President Bill Clinton's lack of action caused nuclear weapons to be built by North Korea. Bill Clinton was in office from Jan. 1993 to Jan 2001. In

1994, North Korea and the United States formed an agreement where North Korea promised to freeze and eventually dismantle its old nuclear reactors in exchange for aid to build new light-water nuclear reactors.

The escalation in conflict with North Korea seemed to occur when a new president, George W. Bush, said North Korea was part of an "axis of evil" in a speech he gave in January, 2002. North Korea withdrew from the Nuclear Nonproliferation Treaty in 2003, and later that year, was known to be developing nuclear weapons.

Perhaps, it would have been fairer to say that when Clinton was secretary of state, she was dealing with a problem she inherited from the Bush administration, rather than making it sound like she was responsible for the problem. Also, Trump's effort to distort the history of the problem to put blame onto Bill Clinton, was also an attempt by Trump to blame Hillary Clinton by using a guilt by association tactic.

Also, perhaps Trump could have learned something by paying attention to how North Korea reacted to criticism from Bush's "Axis of evil" speech in 2003, before Trump gave his critical speech directed at North Korea in 2017.

On Sep 21, 2017, Kim Jong-un, president of the Democratic Republic of North Korea (DPRK), responded to Trump's UN speech with this statement:

"The speech made by the U.S. president in his maiden address on the UN arena in the prevailing serious circumstances, in which the situation on the Korean peninsula has been rendered tense as never before and is inching closer to a touch-and-go state, is arousing worldwide concern.

"Shaping the general idea of what he would say, I expected he would make stereo-typed, prepared remarks a little different from what he used to utter in his office on the spur of the moment as he had to speak on the world's biggest official diplomatic stage.

"But, far from making remarks of any persuasive power that can be viewed to be helpful to defusing tension, he made unprecedented rude nonsense one has never heard from any of his predecessors.

"A frightened dog barks louder.

"I'd like to advise Trump to exercise prudence in selecting words and to be considerate of whom he speaks to when making a speech in front of the world.

"The mentally deranged behavior of the U.S. president openly expressing on the UN arena the unethical will to "totally destroy" a sovereign state, beyond the boundary of threats of regime change or overturn of social system, makes even those with normal thinking faculty think about discretion and composure.

"His remarks remind me of such words as "political layman" and "political heretic" which were in vogue in reference to Trump during his presidential election campaign.

"After taking office, Trump has rendered the world restless through threats and blackmail against all countries in the world. He is unfit to hold the prerogative of supreme command of a country, and he is surely a rogue and a gangster fond of playing with fire, rather than a politician.

"His remarks which described the U.S. option through straightforward expression of his will have convinced me, rather than frightening or stopping me, that the path I chose is correct and that it is the one I have to follow to the last.

"Now that Trump has denied the existence of and insulted me and my country in front of the eyes of the world and made the most ferocious declaration of a war in history that he would

destroy the DPRK, we will consider with seriousness exercising of a corresponding, highest level of hard-line countermeasure in history.

"Action is the best option in treating the dotard who, hard of hearing, is uttering only what he wants to say.

"As a man representing the DPRK and on behalf of the dignity and honor of my state and people and on my own, I will make the man holding the prerogative of the supreme command in the U.S. pay dearly for his speech calling for totally destroying the DPRK.

"This is not a rhetorical expression loved by Trump.

"I am now thinking hard about what response he could have expected when he allowed such eccentric words to trip off his tongue.

"Whatever Trump might have expected, he will face results beyond his expectation. I will surely and definitely tame the mentally deranged U. S. dotard with fire."

Kim Jong-un's statement used the word "dotard" to describe Trump. According to *Meriam Webster Dictionary,* a dotard is: "A person in dotage, a state or period of senile decay marked by decline of mental poise and alertness."

Kim Jung-un gave a New Year's Day address for 2018 and said *"The entire mainland of the US is within the range of our nuclear weapons and the nuclear button is always on the desk of my office. They should accurately be aware that this is not a threat but a reality."* In response, Trump tweeted *"North Korean Leader Kim Jong-un just stated that the "Nuclear Button is on his desk at all times." Will someone from his depleted and food starved regime please inform him that I too have a Nuclear Button, but it is a much bigger & more powerful one than his, and my Button works!"*

Trump's Response to North Korea's Statement

Trump used deflection and destructive criticism in a series of tweets to respond to Kim Jong-un's statement. Here are some of Trump's tweets:

"Kim Jong Un of North Korea, who is obviously a madman who doesn't mind starving or killing his people, will be tested like never before!" – Sep 22, 2017.

"Why would Kim Jong-un insult me by calling me "old," when I would NEVER call him "short and fat?" Oh well, I try so hard to be his friend - and maybe someday that will happen!" – Nov 7, 2017.

"NoKo has interpreted America's past restraint as weakness. This would be a fatal miscalculation. Do not underestimate us. AND DO NOT TRY US." – Nov 8, 2017.

"The weapons you are acquiring are not making you safer, they are putting your regime in grave danger. North Korea is not the paradise your grandfather envisioned, it is a hell that no person deserves, yet despite every crime you have committed against God and man ...we are ready to offer a path to a much better future... Every step you take down this dark path increases the peril you face." – Nov 8, 2017.

Here are things other people have said about how Trump has handled North Korea:

"We are concerned that the President of the United States is so unstable, is so volatile, and has a decision-making process that is so quixotic that he might order a nuclear weapons strike that is wildly out of step with U.S. security interests." – Senator Chris Murphy, Nov 14, 2017

"I have a message for Cadet Bone Spurs [Donald Trump]: If you cared about our military, you'd stop baiting Kim Jong-un into a war that could put 85,000 American troops, and millions of innocent civilians, in danger." - Senator Tammy Duckworth, Jan 21, 2018

"I don't think bragging about whose button is bigger accomplishes anything good... I hope the president finds another way to conduct diplomacy." – Senator Flake, January 2018

These tweets are from Donald Trump:

"Are you allowed to impeach a president for gross incompetence?" – June 4, 2014

"Be prepared, there is a small chance that our horrendous leadership could unknowingly lead us into World War III – Aug 31, 2015

CASINO USA

A ROLL OF THE DICE
A HOUSE OF CARDS
A PAIR OF SNAKE EYES

Nuclear Bomb Risks and Military Costs

If Donald Trump decided to launch nuclear missiles, the whole process may take around fifteen minutes. Once missiles are launched, that decision cannot be undone. If this were to occur, missiles would likely be launched by the other side against the U.S.

Within 40 minutes of a decision to launch missiles, millions and perhaps hundreds of millions of people would die.

Not only would nuclear bombs devastate the cities affected, but the detonation of nuclear bombs could have global consequences. The fallout from the firestorms could alter global weather patterns and cause a reduction in food production around the world. Within a few months of a nuclear war, global food reserves could be depleted and a global famine could kill over a billion people. A global famine caused by nuclear bomb disruptions of weather patterns could last over a decade.

There are approximately 15,000 nuclear bombs in the world and it may take the detonation of only 50 of them to alter weather patterns enough to cause a global famine.

Malfunctions and errors are significant risks for nuclear weapons. On numerous occasions, problems have occurred that could have caused a nuclear catastrophe. The military calls those incidents "broken arrows." For example, there have been occasions where nuclear bombs were accidently dropped from military planes and there have been planes carrying nuclear bombs that have crashed. Also, a nuclear missile silo exploded when a mechanic accidently dropped a socket and it punctured the missile's fuel tank.

Some deaths and injuries have occurred in these incidents and sometimes the only thing that has prevented massive casualties is luck. Officially, there have been 33 broken arrows reported, but many more have likely occurred. Because of the secrecy of the military, sometimes the public never becomes aware of the problems or it only hears of some problems decades after they have occurred.

There have also been numerous instances of security breaches involving nuclear weapons. In addition, at least 6 nuclear weapons have been lost at sea and never recovered.

Even if we never detonate another nuclear bomb, that doesn't mean these weapons don't have consequences. Weapons are expensive to build and maintain. The military is known for its excessive cost overruns and has spent billions on weapons that don't work. The United States is spending $1.6 trillion on major weapon systems and it is estimated that 25% of that spending is for cost overruns.

The cost of building and maintaining weapons and militaries has a significant impact on economic resources around the world. It's estimated the world spends $1.7 trillion each year on military costs. Countries that spend large amounts on defense budgets have less money available to spend on other areas and there is often a reduction in the quality of life for the citizens of countries that spend large amounts on military resources.

Nuclear Weapons (10)
www.BluntHonest.com/Nuclear

Military Costs Versus Quality of Life (10)
www.BluntHonest.com/Military

The World Is a Time Bomb

"The greater danger for most of us lies not in setting our aim too high and falling short, but in setting our aim too low, and achieving our mark." – Michelangelo

"Go big or go extinct."- Movie - Pacific Rim

Our world is an amazing place. It's unlikely that we'll find or visit any other planet as special as this in our lifetime. This planet is the only home we have. Yet, at times, it seems as though we treat this treasure trove of life as though it is trash. It took 4.5 billion years for life on this planet to evolve. In the span of less than 100 years, humans have put this world in danger of being lost because of the harm we are causing.

Far too often, we put our selfish interests ahead of the good of our world. We are our own worst enemies. We are the greatest risk to ourselves. The most significant problems we face are related to our combined lack of empathy and our failure to perceive reality. Our selfish interests are crippling our ability, and our will, to do what is best for all of us. We can't see the big picture because we get caught up in our distorted perceptions of the world and ignore the reality of the harm we are causing.

In some ways, our world is like a ticking time bomb. As long as our ability to destroy one another exceeds our ability to understand each other, then at any given moment nuclear weapons could destroy this planet at the whim of an irrational leader or by malfunction or errors.

If weapons of mass destruction don't kill us, then climate change may lead to the end of life on this planet as we know it. Since the 1950's, scientists have been warning us that carbon dioxide produced by burning fossil fuels is harming the environment. Attempts to solve this problem have been restricted by lobbying efforts and false information being spread by wealthy and powerful industries that pollute the environment.

The rational choices are to eliminate weapons of mass destruction, reduce our military expenses, and put our resources toward reducing the harm we are causing to the environment. This planet will survive with or without us. We aren't saving the planet, we are saving ourselves.

There seems to be a disconnect between our minds and our hearts. We know what our problems are and we know we need to do something. Yet we lack the courage and passion to take action. We need to find the place inside of us that makes us great. Humans are at their best when their minds and hearts align.

In this book, I've appealed to your mind and your heart. Videos connect with us in ways that books cannot. Videos help share empathy and emotions. When words are in a song, the effect of those words is different than if the same words are put on the pages of a book. Books speak to our minds and poems sing to our souls. Songs are poetry.

The following video montages show important issues and these montages encourage people to come together to resolve the issues. Please share these links with others.

Our World & Hopes for the Future (10)
www.BluntHonest.com/World

Challenge to Life - Climate Change (10)
www.BluntHonest.com/Life

Creativity and Diversity

Every day, our lives are affected by millions of people. For example, consider how a smartphone uses ideas from over 250,000 patents. The components of phones have evolved over thousands of years. The camera on your smartphone has origins going back to 3,500 BCE when Egyptians discovered how to make glass. Around 750 BCE Assyrians began experimenting with optics. Around 500 BCE the Chinese were using camera obscuras.

Some of the manufacturing processes used to create your phone go back to 5000 BCE when blacksmiths in Serbia began smelting metal. Mathematics started in the 6th century BCE and today engineering and software rely upon math. Mechanical and electronic computing has matured over the centuries into modern computers. Plastic was developed in 1907 and has evolved. Software, hardware, electrical grids, worldwide networks, and space satellites are used by your phone. A global, cooperative effort of people from around the world and throughout the ages have made your smartphone possible.

Your smartphone is millions of times more powerful than the room full of large computers used to put men on the moon in the Apollo program. Around 400,000 people worked on the Apollo program. The accomplishments of those 400,000 people have made some of the technology used by your phone possible.

Many of the things we experience today were created from the cooperation of generations of people with diverse talents and backgrounds. For example, flying in an airplane is the result of the ideas and efforts of tens of millions of people.

Our minds are different from one other. We may not understand how another's mind works, or even understand each other's ideas, yet we find ways to respect and appreciate each other's talents. Our diversity makes us strong. When we work together, we can accomplish great things. We have the ability to solve our problems. We just have to do it.

Creativity of Mankind (8, 9)
www.BluntHonest.com/Creativity

Evolution of Flight (7, 8)
www.BluntHonest.com/Flight

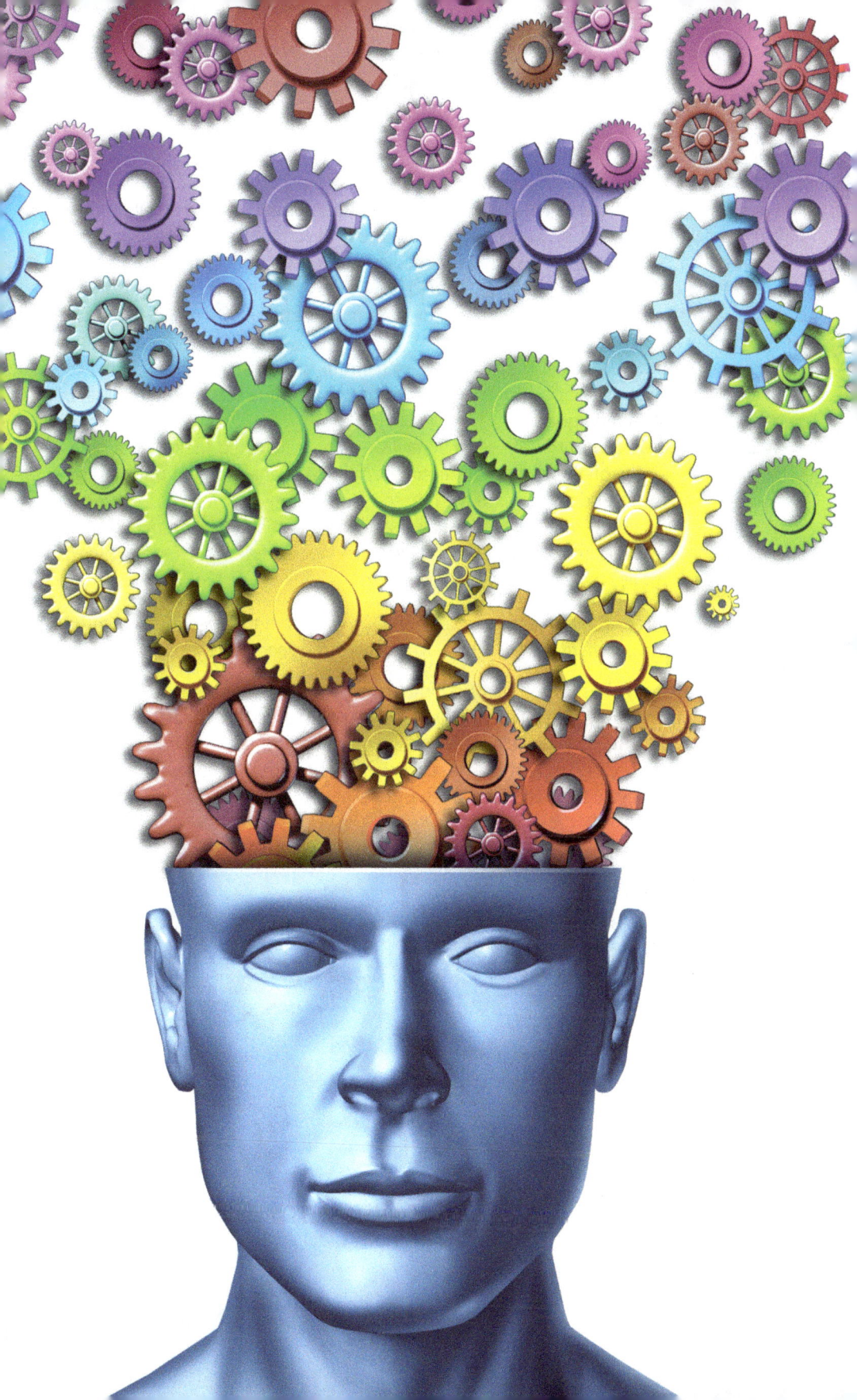

The Benefits of Viruses

In a person's body, cells have defensive mechanisms to protect them from disease and illness. However, some viruses are able to bypass the defenses and enter the cells. It can be difficult to deliver medicine into the cells because the cells sometimes reject the medicine.

Scientists have found that they can attach medicine to a virus and use the virus to bypass a cell's defense mechanisms. This allows them to deliver the medicine into the cell so that the cell accepts the medicine. Even though a virus is normally harmful to a cell, in some cases viruses can serve as tools to help the cells.

Toxic people are like viruses. They can be very harmful to us, but at the same time they have a way of forcing us to open our minds and cause us to self-reflect and reconsider our beliefs, values, history, and goals.

When I was dealing with the abuse of an evil woman, it launched me down a path of self-discovery and personal growth that might not have happened if I had not met her. It took me a while to see and understand the role she played in my life.

The abuse and harm of that woman was like a shadow that stayed with me long after she was gone. But over time, I learned and grew from that experience. One day I had an interesting thought as I reflected on that experience:

Life is a series of silver-lined paradoxes. Sometimes you have to meet the Antichrist to help you find Jesus. Sometimes in life you have to accept the good with the bad and the ugly.

In history, after an abusive person or regime affects society, there tends to be a period of reconciliation and growth that comes from a reevaluation of societal beliefs and goals.

Perhaps Donald Trump will make America great again in a way that is different from what his supporters were hoping for. Perhaps he will make America great again by forcing people to self-reflect and reevaluate their core values and beliefs.

Trumpus Influenza
(Magnified a Gazillion Times)

We Need to Talk About Donald

"As democracy is perfected, the office of president represents, more and more closely, the inner soul of the people. On some great day the plain folks of the land will reach their heart's desire at last, and the White House will be adorned by a downright moron." — H.L. Mencken, July 26, 1920

It is usually best to avoid all contact with a narcissist. However, someone who may have a big impact on your life is hard to ignore. So, what can you do?

Logic doesn't work very well with narcissists because they are often illogical. It's hard to reason with someone who is so unreasonable. Criticism doesn't work with narcissists, even if it is constructive feedback. Anything that feels like criticism may cause them to lash out and attack whoever provides the criticism. Shame doesn't work on narcissists because they lack empathy and don't have much of a conscience. A narcissist will likely flip things around and use shame and blame tactics on whoever tries to get a narcissist to self-reflect.

You may be able to manage a narcissist by stroking their ego and being careful what you say to them. They need to feel like they are in control and that they are the focus of your attention. Relationships with narcissists are not reciprocal and are draining. You can appease a narcissist and give them whatever they want in order to avoid their temper tantrums. However, this can feel like you are a parent who has a child like Damien from the movie *The Omen*.

No matter how careful you are, it's only a matter of time before you injure the fragile ego of a narcissist and a fight breaks out. Also, narcissists don't fight fairly. Nothing is worth all the crazy drama a narcissist brings into your world. Any form of conflict or disagreement seems to energize a narcissist. They seem to look for excuses to cause drama storms.

As you can see, narcissists are slippery, slimy birds. Trying to change a narcissist is like trying to put lipstick on a pig. George Bernard Shaw wisely said *"I learned long ago, never to wrestle with a pig. You get dirty, and besides, the pig likes it."* Narcissists get their energy by stealing your energy.

If you can't avoid a narcissist, about the only thing you can do to handle a narcissist is to use the "Gray Rock" method. This means you become as boring as a stone and show no reaction to the craziness of a narcissist. When you have no reaction to a narcissist, there is no energy for them to feed on. It is hard for a narcissist to create a drama storm when nobody shows up to participate.

When it comes to Trump, most of us have no contact with him and seemingly no way to influence him. However, Trump has a weakness that is common among narcissists. In fact, Trump showed his weakness while he was running for president.

During the presidential campaign, Trump was calling Marco Rubio "Little Marco." One day Rubio was talking to a crowd about Trump and said *"He is taller than me, he's like 6' 2", which is why I don't understand why his hands are the size of someone who is 5' 2". Have you seen his hands? And you know what they say about men with small hands... you can't trust them."*

After Rubio said that Trump's hands were small, Trump brought this up many times during the campaign and showed people his "big hands." Even after he was president, Trump continued to show his hands and tell people he has big hands.

Graydon Carter, editor of Vanity Fair magazine, wrote an article in *Spy* magazine in 1988 that described Trump as a *"short-fingered vulgarian."* Almost 30 years has passed since he wrote that, but in November, 2015, Carter said *"To this day, I receive the occasional envelope from Trump. There is always a photo of him—generally a tear sheet from a magazine. On all of them he has circled his hand in gold Sharpie in a valiant effort to highlight the length of his fingers...also written in gold Sharpie: 'See, not so short!'"*

In 1964, Donald Trump attended the grand opening ceremony of the Verrazano-Narrow's Bridge. At that event, the designer of the bridge did not get the recognition Trump felt he deserved. Trump later told a reporter *"I realized then and there that if you let people treat you how they want, you'll be made a fool. I realized then and there something I would never forget: I don't want to be made anybody's sucker."*

Trump's weakness is that he needs to feel important. He doesn't want to be ignored. He especially doesn't want to feel like he is the punchline of a joke. Trump's desire to not be a fool sometimes causes him to overreact and look like a fool. He overacted when he was the punchline of Bill Maher's orangutan joke. Trump also overreacted when John Stewart gave him a nickname of "F**kface Von Clownstick."

When people stop taking narcissists seriously they become disarmed. They become like the Grinch who tried to steal Christmas but couldn't because nobody paid attention to him.

The real Donald Trump is like the animatronic version of him at Disney World. He operates according to how you push his buttons. His mind is triggered by reactions that launch psychological schemas inside of him. Often, he is running on auto-pilot. He isn't consciously thinking about what he says and does. Instead of using self-reflection and reasoning to guide him, he operates on impulses. He lacks awareness and mindfulness. He is more like a maniac robot than a human being.

When you look past the false façade of a narcissist and peer into their soul you'll understand that they are nothing but smoke and mirrors and hot air. They have no substance. They are like an emperor who has no clothes.

Donald Trump is like a pompous wizard of Oz trying to convince the world that he is a great and powerful leader. But when you look behind the curtain, he is merely a spoiled, rich kid who likes to misbehave, and who enjoys treating others like puppets. Let's treat Donald like the silly clown he is. Trump is not a real president. He only plays one on TV. He is a Quack. Trump is merely Donald the duck with tiny hands.

Lame Duck

KING DONALD'S GLOBAL MISADVENTURES
Hey Kids! (and kids at heart)

Send King Donald on a trip around the globe!

Color and decorate King Donald. Cut him out and send him to friends, family, and world leaders everywhere. Ask them to post pictures with themselves and King Donald online. Take King Donald any place the real Donald is creating chaos and let others know he is like an emperor without clothes.

Photograph and share this image or visit www.DuckPrez.com/Flat for pictures of Flat Donald you can print and share.

DUCKPREZ.com

Do You Like COLORING BOOKS?

We made a coloring book that you'll enjoy.

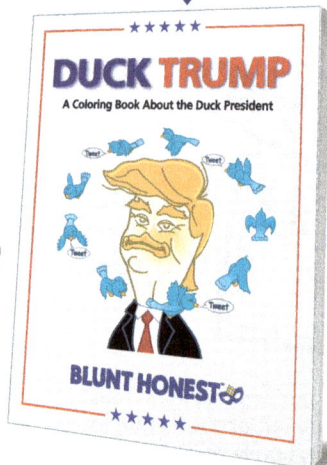

POSTCARDS

We offer 60 color postcard designs
based on the illustrations in this book.
Postcards available at **DuckPrez.com**

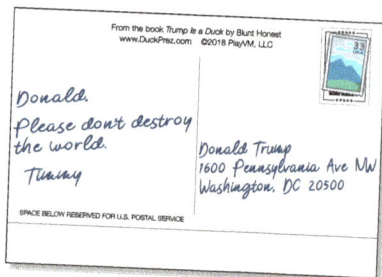

The backside of each postcard has
plenty of room to write a message.

DUCKPREZ.com

Test Your Knowledge

This crossword puzzle is based on things Donald Trump said and news stories about him.

Across:
1. What president is a stable genius with a high IQ?
2. Name the president who is victimized by "Fake News."
3. Who can do anything he wants to women, because he is a star?
4. Who is the Hemmingway of Twitter?
5. Who is *"The greatest single president in the history of our country"* according to Trump?
6. Based on a 2018 survey of 170 political scientists, who is the worst president of all time?
7. Name the person (or his company) who have been involved in over 3,500 lawsuits.
8. Who sued the comedian Bill Maher for $5 million for telling a joke about an orangutan?
9. Who said his sex life was like being a brave soldier in the Vietnam War?

Down:
1. Who said he has *"one of the greatest memories of all time?"*
2. Who said he *"couldn't remember"* 59 times during 2 lawsuits?
3. Who tweeted *"we could use a little bit of the good old global warming?"*
4. Who displayed fake *Time* magazine covers with his face on it at his golf resorts?
5. Who prefers people from Norway over people from *"Shithole"* countries?
6. Who told reporters he is the least racist person?
7. What president went golfing 95 times during his first year in office?
8. In the 2016 presidential election, who won the popular vote by 2,864,974 votes?

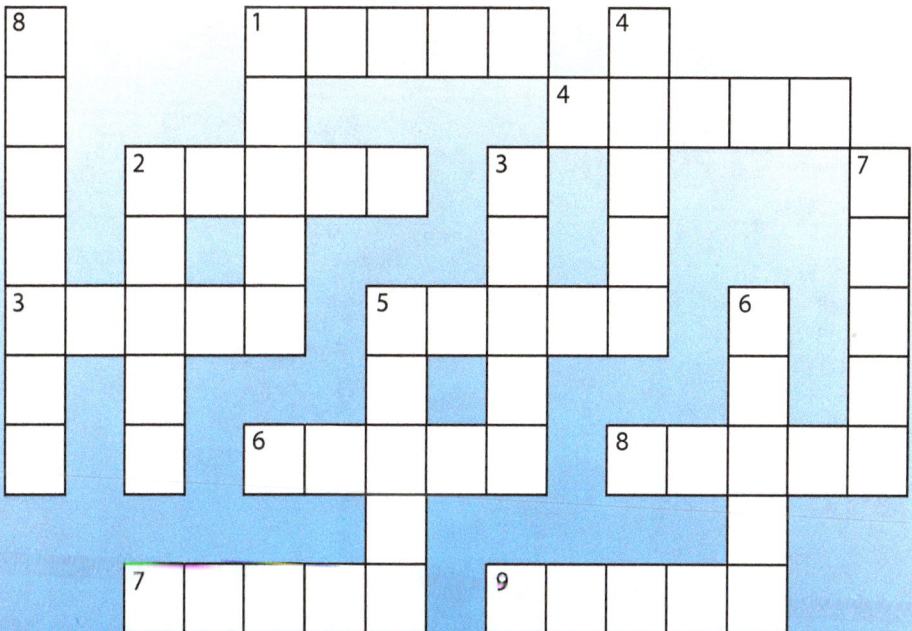

Answers: TRUMP is the answer for all items, except for 8 Down the answer is CLINTON

How Many Lies Are Hidden in This Picture?

He didn't do anything wrong.

He begged me.

My wires were tapped.

I don't remember.

She was more popular because of voter fraud.

I'm going to drain the swamp.

This is the worst ever...

I will make Mexico pay for the wall.

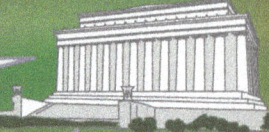

Fake news!

Biggest inauguration crowd ever.

This is the single greatest...

This is a witch hunt

Tax Reform will cost me a fortune.

I never met her

Answer: 4,229

According to *The Washington Post*, Trump made 4,229 untrue or misleading statements during his first 558 days in office. He makes around 7.6 false claims per day.

Trump's Monikers and Insults

Donald Trump frequently uses nicknames to criticize people, places, and organizations. Here are some of the put-downs that Trump has reportedly said:

1 for 38
13 Angry Democrats
A No-Talent Guy
Al Frankenstien
Amazon Washington Post
Animal Assad
Average Talent
Chained Lunatic
Cheatin' Obama
Clinton News Network
Crazy Bernie
Crazy Jim
Crazy Joe
Crazy Megyn
Cried Like a Baby
Crooked H Flunkie
Crooked Hillary
Cryin Chuck
Deadpan George
Deface the Nation
Dicky Durbin
Dishonest Press
Dopey Arianna
Dopey Bill
Dopey Chicago Tribune
Dopey Clown Mort
Dopey Eric
Dopey George
Dopey Graydon
Dopey Jon
Dopey Karl
Dopey Lawrence
Dopey Mark
Dopey Megyn
Dopey Prince
Dopey Rosie
Dopey Sugar
Dumb as a Rock
Dumbest Man on Television
Dummy Angelo

Dummy Arianna
Dummy Chuck
Dummy Clare
Dummy Graydon
Dummy Mark
Dummy Reporter John
Extremely Unattractive
Failing Host
Failing WSJ
Fake Tears Schumer
Goofball
Haters and Losers
Head Clown
Heartless Hillary
Highly Untalented
Jeff Flakey
Lamb the Sham
Leakin' James
Liddle Bob
Lightweight Senator
Little Adam
Little George
Little Jeff
Little Katy
Little Marco
Little Rocket Man
Lonely, Miserable Loser
Look at that Face
Low Energy Jeb
Low-IQ Individual
Low Life Dummy
Lyin' Hillary
Lyin' Ted
Lying James
Mad Alex
McMuffin
Mental Basketcase
Mexican Judge
Miss Piggy
Moonbeam

Mr Magoo
Overrated
Pocahontas
Psycho Joe
Puppet Jones
Sanctimonious James
Shady James
Shithole Countries
Should be Ashamed
Sir Charles
Sleepin' Joe
Sleepy Eyes
Slippery James
Sloppy Michael
Sloppy Steve
Sneaky Dianne
So-Called Judge
Stupid George
Third Rate
Too Easy-Danny
Total Fool Karl
Total Joke
Totally Unhinged
Unsexiest
Very Fake News
Wacky Wilson
Wild Bill

Moniker Maker Tool

Trump seems to use many of the same words in his monikers. Perhaps he is running out of words. It must be stressful for a genius like Trump to use his valuable non-golfing time to come up with new monikers. To help Trump, I have created a tool he can use to generate monikers and expand his vocabulary. Here are some moniker-worthy words from A to Z.

Aberrant	Clueless	Grouchy	Pansy	Toxic
Abusive	Clumsy	Grumpy	Paranoid	Train Wreck
Abysmal	Cockroach	Guilty	Parasite	Traitor
Acid	Con Artist	Gullible	Pig	Trash
Afraid	Cranky	Half-Baked	Piranha	Troll
Airhead	Crazy	Hooligan	Pretentious	Trump
Alien	Creepy	Hussy	Prick	Trumpian
Anathema	Cuckoo	Hypocrite	Prissy	Trumpty Dumpty
Anemic	Culprit	Hysterical	Pushover	Turkey
Ape	Dabbler	Idiot	Quack	Tutti-Frutti
Arm Candy	Daffy	Imbecile	Quirky	Two Faced
Arrogant	Desperate	Inept	Recluse	Ugly
Awful	Detestable	Insane	Redneck	Unremarkable
Bad Apple	Deviant	Jackass	Repugnant	Unsavory
Baldy	Dimwit	Jaded	Repulsive	Untrustworthy
Banana	Dingbat	Jerk	Ridiculous	Unworthy
Bashful	Disgusting	Joker	Rodent	Uppity
Berserk	Ditsy	Killer	Rotten Egg	Vain
Big Headed	Dork	Kinky	Scam Artist	Vampire
Bigmouth	Dotard	Kitschy	Scammer	Vile
Bilker	Drama	Kooky	Scoundrel	Village Idiot
Blabby	Dreadful	Lacky	Scrooge	Villain
Boor	Drumpf	Lazy	Scum	Wanker
Bogus	Dunce	Leaker	Shallow	Weakling
Bonehead	Easy	Loser	Shark	Weasel
Boring	Eccentric	Low Class	Sheisty	Weenie
Bossy	Eerie	Megalomaniac	Silly	Weepy
Brainiac	Egotistical	Miser	Slouchy	Whack Job
Brainless	Enigma	Misfit	Sneezy	Whiner
Bridezilla	Evil	Monster	Sniffy	Worm
Buffoon	Eyeful	Moocher	Space Cadet	Wreck
Bully	Fake	Motley	Spoiled	Wuss
Bum	Fool	Narcissist	Stingy	Wussy
Butthead	Frenemy	Nasty	Stuffy	Xenophobic
Cadet	Frigid	Nemesis	Stupid	X-Rated
Caveman	Fruitcake	Nincompoop	Substandard	Yahoo
Chameleon	Frumpy	Nut Job	Suspicious	Yellow
Charlatan	Fungus	Obnoxious	Tacky	Yucky
Cheapskate	Gangster	Orangutan	Thoughtless	Zany
Cheater	Gold Digger	Orwellian	Timid	Zero
Chump	Goon	Outrageous	Tiny	Zilch
Clown	Greedy	Over Rated	Tired	Zombie

A Moniker for Trump

Donald Trump likes to invent monikers to describe people, especially people who are his opponents and people he doesn't like. So many people have been given derogatory nicknames by Trump that the words and tweets coming out of his mouth are becoming a farce. Donald Trump is like an old corroded pot calling a stainless-steel kettle black.

When Trump gives someone a moniker it's almost like receiving a badge of honor. When Trump gave Senator Feinstein the nickname of "Sneaky," Democratic Leader Nancy Pelosi sent out a tweet congratulating Feinstein for earning a Trump nickname because that means she is *"Clearly doing something right."*

Nancy Pelosi has called Trump "Ronald McDonald" because he is such a clown and he eats a lot of hamburgers. When Trump bragged about his Nuclear Button on his desk, KFC in UK & Ireland, laid down the gauntlet against Ronald McDonald and sent out this tweet:

"McDonald's leader Ronald just stated he has a "burger on his desk at all times. Will someone from his big-shoed, red-nosed regime inform him that I too have a burger on my desk, but mine is a box meal which is bigger and more powerful than his, and mine has gravy!"

All this childish tit-for-tat behavior brings back fond memories of my days in kindergarten and has inspired me to come up with a moniker for Trump.

After considering how Trump lacks empathy, is disrespectful of others, distorts the truth, always needs to be the center of attention, has an over-inflated ego, deflects responsibility, and enjoys causing unnecessary conflict and drama, the best way to describe Trump is:

Trump is a Dick

But as I thought more about this, I realized there were some problems with using "Dick" as his moniker. First of all, I would not want to offend people who are named Richard. Second, Trump might consider "Dick" to be a compliment about his manhood. Also, there are a finite number of ways to tastefully present dick images or to tell dick jokes. In addition, the audience for shirts and other products with phallic symbols might be somewhat limited. I decided the best way to describe him that would also have a wider appeal would be to say:

Trump is a Duck

That moniker for Trump inspired the title of this book and the cartoons in this book.

Trump's Character Traits (7,8)
www.BluntHonest.com/Trump

DON'T BE A DUCK

I Have a Nuclear Button…

Now everybody can have a nuclear button on their desk. To help save the world, we are offering personal nuclear buttons to the public. Many styles and options are available.

We offer nuclear buttons that create the sound of a bomb siren when it is pushed. We also offer buttons with a flashing red light to warn people you are about to go nuclear if they don't treat you better.

Some nuclear buttons conceal other tools such as drink coasters or mirrors. Some nuclear buttons have magnets to attach them to your refrigerator or other metal surfaces. One style of button is on a keychain and contains a bottle opener. There are safety pins on some buttons so that you can wear a nuclear button on your chest at all times. Or perhaps you'd like to wear it on your hat, on a backpack, or use it as a tie clasp.

We also offer missiles to help you feel safer. Our missiles look like magnetic darts and we offer a variety of targets you can use to test your missiles.

Think how safe the world will become once everyone has a nuclear button. People will be forced to be nice to each other or risk being annihilated. These nuclear buttons will bring about peace and harmony on Earth because everyone will respect each other. Goodwill shall spread across mankind after everyone has a nuclear button.

For women, these buttons are an important part of your personal security regiment. For men, there is no better way to demonstrate your high level of testosterone to attract a potential mate.

You will want to own several buttons. One for your home and one for work. One to keep in your car and another for your bomb shelter. Be sure to take a button to the gym and shopping mall and anywhere else a conflict might develop. It is not enough to just have one nuclear button. The more you have the safer you will feel.

Do your part to save the world. Order your nuclear buttons and missiles today. To see the wide variety of personal nuclear buttons and missiles available, visit:

www.DuckPrez.com

Most of the Illustrations from this book are available on shirts, hats, posters, signs, stickers, buttons, magnets, key chains, bottle openers, magnetic dart boards, coffee mugs, playing cards, throwing discs, and more. To see available products, visit **www.DuckPrez.com**

Make America Safe Again

As you can see, we have a duck in the White House. As long as that duck is mismanaging the country, America and the world are at risk.

I am launching a campaign to "Get Out the Duck." It is an eviction campaign to get that duck out of the White House. Let's put an end to this duck's dynasty. Let's make America safe again. Once we've recovered from the regime of the duck, America will be great again.

Not everyone knows that we have a duck in the White House. Let's raise the awareness of this issue. Once more people are aware of this situation, then it's only a matter of time before that duck is forced to leave his keys at the door.

Please tell others about this book. Also, the website DuckPrez.com has a variety of products and tools to help spread the word that Donald Trump is a duck. In addition, DuckPrez.com offers free flyers you can print and hang in public places. There are also images and videos provided for you to share on social media. Please do your part to help save the world by letting others know that we have a duck in the White House.

All of the products on DuckPrez.com make excellent gifts for people who don't like Trump. Those products also make great gifts for Trump supporters because they need to be woken up. You may want to send this book to your representatives in Congress. Probably the biggest Trump supporter is Donald Trump, himself. He definitely needs to be woken up.

Trump has a birthday coming up on June 14, and this book or any of the items on DuckPrez.com, are great gifts to send him. Also, you don't have to wait for Donald Trump's birthday to send him a gift. The next page shows other great occasions to send a gift to Donald Trump.

When lots of people send gifts to Trump, he will realize that we know the truth about him. Perhaps this will encourage him to resign or cause him to spontaneously combust in a fit of narcissistic rage. Here are some addresses you can use to send your gifts to Donald Trump:

Donald Trump	Donald Trump	Donald Trump
The White House	Mar-a-Lago Club	Trump Tower
1600 Pennsylvania Ave NW	1100 S Ocean Blvd	725 5th Ave
Washington, DC 20500	Palm Beach, FL 33480	New York, NY 10022

Die-cut vinyl stickers are available for indoor or outdoor use. Stickers can be purchased at DuckPrez.com

Great Occasions to Send Gifts to Trump

Polar Bear Plunge Day (Jan 1)
Russian Orthodox Christmas (Jan 7)
Squirrel Appreciation Day (Jan 21)
Lame Duck Day (Feb 6)
National Pizza Day (Feb 9)
National Mistress Day (Feb 13)
Do A Grouch a Favor Day (Feb 16)
Random Act of Kindness Day (Feb 17)
Presidents Day (Feb 19)
Be Humble Day (Feb 22)
No Brainer Day (Feb 22)
World Compliment Day (Mar 1)
International Woman's Day (Mar 8)
Everything You Think Is Wrong Day (Mar 15)
Awkward Moments Day (Mar 18)
International Goof Off Day (Mar 22)
Smoke and Mirrors Day (Mar 29)
April Fool's Day (Apr 1)
Tell a Lie Day (Apr 4)
Be Kind to Lawyers Day (Apr 10)
Earth Day (Apr 22),
Honesty Day (Apr 30)
National Postcard Week (First week of May)
Cinco De Mayo (May 5)
Eat What You Want Day (May 11)
Ramadan (May 15)
Be a Millionaire Day (May 20)
Hamburger Day (May 28)
Say Something Nice Day (Jun 1)
World Narcissistic Abuse Awareness Day (Jun 1)
Donald Duck Day (Jun 9)
Eat Your Vegetables Day (Jun 17)
International Panic Day (Jun 18)
Juneteenth (June 19)
Gay Pride Month (June)
Please Take My Children to Work Day (Jun 25)
Compliment Your Mirror Day (Jul 3)

Independence Day (Jul 4)
Tell the Truth Day (Jul 7)
National Junk Food Day (Jul 21)
National Coloring Book Day (Aug 2)
Happiness Happens Day (Aug 8)
Frankenstein Day (Aug 30)
No Rhyme or Reason Day (Sep 1)
Pardon Day (Sep 8)
Positive Thinking Day (Sep 13)
National Clean Up Day (Sep 15)
International Talk like a Pirate Day (Sep 19)
Miniature Golf Day (Sep 21)
International Day of Peace (Sept 21)
Ask a Stupid Question Day (Sep 28)
International Postcard Week (Early October)
World Smile Day (Oct 5)
Mad Hatter Day (Oct 6)
Curious Events Day (Oct 9)
International Skeptics Day (Oct 13)
International Sloth Day (Oct 20)
Count Your Buttons Day (Oct 21)
Halloween (Oct 31)
Common Sense Day (Nov 4)
Guy Fawkes Day (Nov 5)
Chaos Never Dies Day (Nov 9)
World Kindness Day (Nov 13)
Fast Food Day (Nov 16)
National Absurdity Day (Nov 20)
Start Your Own Country Day (Nov 22)
National Day of Listening (Nov 23)
Hanukkah (Dec 2)
National Miner's Day (Dec 6)
Monkey Day (Dec 14)
Festivus (Dec 23)
Christmas (Dec 25)
Kwanzaa (Dec 26)
Make Up Your Mind Day (Dec 31)

PRISONER
8645
TRUMP, DONALD J.

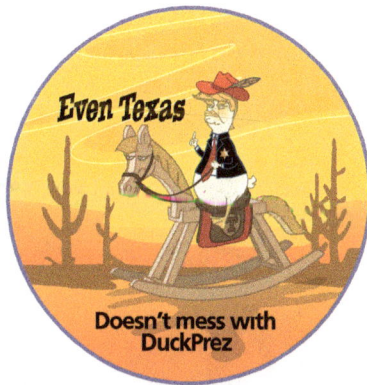

Even Texas

Doesn't mess with
DuckPrez

Don't Be the Last Kid on the Block

This is my first book in a series of books about life and about our world. I also plan to launch projects to make a difference in the world that you can participate in. Let's stay in touch and over time I'll share some great ideas, knowledge, cool stuff, and interesting and fun experiences. I also have more video montages to share.

If you don't subscribe to my newsletter and follow me online, then someday you may end up feeling like the last kid on the block whose family got a color television. If you were born after 1980 then you probably don't know what black and white televisions were. So, for you, if you don't follow me to stay in touch, then someday you may feel like the last kid on the block whose family got a PlayStation, Xbox, or a smartphone.

You'll especially want to follow me if you live anywhere near the planet Earth. To subscribe to my newsletter, visit: **www.BluntHonest.com**

For those of you who explored the depths of this book by watching the video montages and reading the information, perhaps you've come to realize that this book is a rabbit hole and you are Alice.

Your Influence Is Important

Each of us have the ability to influence others and our combined influence can change things and make a positive difference in this world. Please tell others about this book and post your reviews online. Some great websites for posting reviews include Amazon, Goodreads, and Barnes and Noble. When talking about this book on Twitter, please use #TrumpDuckBook

There may be people who haven't read this book who will post negative reviews to discourage others from reading my book. Your review is important because it can help counterbalance the reviews posted by non-readers. Thank you for reading this book and for telling others about it.

Also, I've provided images and videos on my website that you can share on Twitter, Instagram, Facebook, Pinterest, or other social media. To use that content, visit:

www.BluntHonest.com/Share

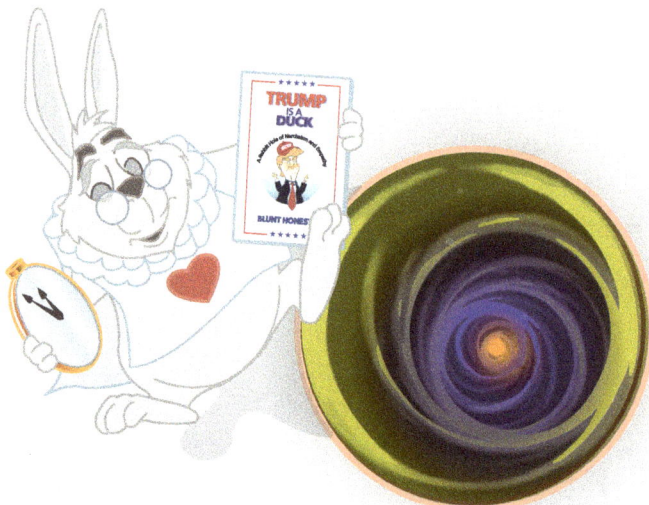

Around the World

"Travel is fatal to prejudice, bigotry, and narrow-mindedness, and many of our people need it sorely on these accounts. Broad, wholesome, charitable views of men and things cannot be acquired by vegetating in one little corner of the Earth all one's lifetime." - Mark Twain

When you spend time with people from other parts of the world, you realize that people are similar in many ways. Regardless of where we are from, we care about our families and our homes. We care about our health and the future. We want to live in peace. We care about animals, especially our pets. We want to be respected and treated fairly. All of us, as humans, share many of the same hopes and dreams. Once you realize this, it becomes easier to appreciate how each of us is also special and unique.

Travel helps us to see how extraordinary the Earth is. This planet is a precious gift that we all share. It belongs to all of us, not only humans but animals as well. It took billions of years to create this place and it is irreplaceable. It's something we should cherish and protect. Our ability to cooperate and respect each other, and to strive for the greater good for all of us, will determine the course of our future.

Around the World in 80 Minutes (8, 9)
www.BluntHonest.com/Around

Nature Is Fascinating (8, 9)
www.BluntHonest.com/Nature

Authentic Anarchy

The Authentic Anarchy movement was founded by Blunt Honest. This is a peaceful movement, but that doesn't mean it is passive or boring. Authentic Anarchy appeals to the hearts and minds of caring people by using creativity, intelligence, and humor to draw attention to important issues and disrupt and change the status quo..

For more information about this movement, or to order a cool shirt, visit:
www.AuthenticAnarchy.com

Seven Deadly Sins

LUST

PRIDE

GREED

ENVY

GLUTTONY

WRATH

SLOTH

Official Presidential Flag

This is the official flag of the Duck President with 30 iconic images of him.

A poster of this flag is available at **DuckPrez.com**

www.ingramcontent.com/pod-product-compliance
Lightning Source LLC
Chambersburg PA
CBHW050744030426
42336CB00012B/1641